P9-AFF-248

PRAISE FOR SUE FREDERICK'S WORK

"Sue Frederick's powerful intuitive techniques have rocked my world both professionally and personally. True love is indeed waiting for each of us, but first we must honor our own unique gifts. Sue's work has helped me open the door for my soul mate to enter and stand beside me. She can help you do the same!"   —*Kim Shannon, author of* The SHINE Cards: 123 Aspects of What It Means to Be a Woman

"Until I met Sue, I was pretty sure that intuition was a 'woman thing,' and I clearly was not a participant. With the intuitive insight I received from Sue's guidance, I have come to realize that we are all gifted with the same access to an intuitive self that most of us barely know. Now when I speak to groups, I remind everyone that if they think about it, they are familiar with that intuitive voice—it's the one they have spent their entire lives trying to outwit, outsmart, and override. Sue helped me to understand that I am not smarter than my intuition and that by ignoring it I was passing up the best guidance, direction, and focus I would ever encounter."   —*Ken Ludwig, host of* What We're Talking About radio show *and director of Red Door Sanctuary in Denver*

"Working with Sue is like having direct access to the divine wisdom that is trying to guide your life in the best direction. Sue's insight and wisdom leaves you knowing what you need to do in your life, your work, your relationships. She also teaches you to feel your own inner light, so that you can be your own best teacher. Reading Sue's books and working with her is one of the great blessings of being alive at this time."   —*Katherine Dreyer, co-founder, CEO, ChiLiving, Inc.*

"Sue's work is uniquely insightful and accurate. She's right on target and continues to inspire me!" —*Ingrid Johnson, founder of The Baby Parenting Coach Institute*

"Closing your eyes and seeing and feeling a day of doing the work you imagined you'd like to do—from start to finish—is a powerful compass to help you choose. Sue's work is brilliant!" —*Dana Moorman, Business Development and Leadership Coach*

"After winding down my 15-year-old business, I was exhausted, confused, and uninspired. I found Sue's book, *I See Your Dream Job*, stayed up until 2 A.M. reading it—and e-mailed her to set up a personal consultation (also at 2 A.M.). Her insights about my life's purpose and direction were enlightening, spot-on, and surprising. A year later, I haven't stopped thinking about the conversation and am taking steps to align myself with her recommendations." —*Marianne Richmond, CEO of marketing company*

"My work with Sue changed my life!! I simply cannot thank her enough for the new perspective she brought to my life story." —*Heather Hans, MSW, psychotherapist*

"Sue provides energetic encouragement and clarity amongst the chaos. She will find your divine direction and teach you to bloom. Highly recommended." —*Vibeke Seymour, global logistics coordinator for manufacturing company*

I SEE YOUR
SOUL MATE

ALSO BY SUE FREDERICK

I See Your Dream Job

I SEE YOUR
SOUL MATE

An Intuitive's Guide to
Finding and Keeping Love

SUE FREDERICK

ST. MARTIN'S PRESS ❧ NEW YORK

I SEE YOUR SOUL MATE. Copyright © 2012 by Sue Frederick.
All rights reserved. Printed in the United States of America.
For information, address St. Martin's Press, 175 Fifth Avenue,
New York, N.Y. 10010.

www.stmartins.com

Book design by Ellen Cipriano

ISBN 978-1-250-00180-1
e-ISBN 978-1-250-01724-6

First Edition: September 2012

10 9 8 7 6 5 4 3 2 1

To Gene,
whose love brought me home

CONTENTS

ACKNOWLEDGMENTS

The 2009 publication of *I See Your Dream Job* hoisted me into the whirlwind of doing my soul's true work, and I've never felt so alive and happy. It's been wonderful to be overwhelmed with clients, students, and book fans who've passionately wanted to learn more about how intuition and birth path reveal our life purpose.

Thank you to every one of you, especially those who allowed me to share your stories in this book and have helped me in numerous other wonderful ways: Kim Shannon, Ken Ludwig, Kat Garrard, Gary Purnhagen, Wendy Snyder, Elizabeth Moore, Felicia Bender, Beth Ellington, Tobi Hunt, Chi Chi Griffin, Angela Vernaglia, Lynn Overton, Joy Brugh, Theresa Shannon, Donna Davis, Marty Traynor, Katherine Dreyer, Barbara Wainwright, Berry Fowler, Gloria Bucco, Bob Goldhamer, and many others that I can't possibly name here—thank you thank you thank you thank you!!!

To my blessed tribe of intuitive coaches whom I've loved teaching, sharing stories with, learning from, and meeting in person wherever I travel—you've filled my life with joy and I feel blessed by your passion, powerful questions, and intense desire to spread this work. You've clarified for me that I love teaching this work beyond doing just about anything else! Without you, this new book would not have been written. There is not enough love and praise in the world to describe how I feel about all of you!

Big huge hugs and kisses to my editor Jennifer Enderlin at St. Martin's Press and my agent Lisa Hagan. You two have truly changed my life!

My deepest gratitude goes to my husband and soul mate Gene, and our two beyond brilliant children—Sarah and Kai. Without our loving home and the great wisdom we share in our rock and roll, theatrical, laughter-filled household, I would not still be doing this.

The more I've done this work in the world, the more powerfully I've appreciated and embraced the ancient intuitive and clairvoyant gifts both parents passed to me through my New Orleans Creole and Irish family lineages. I'm so grateful for the beloved cousins, aunts, uncles, departed grandparents, and all the divine connections that resulted in my blessed birth in that sacred city. To this day, I hold New Orleans in deepest reverence.

As always I offer abundant love and prayer to my posse of divine guides including Nityananda and the many departed loved ones (Paul, Crissie, Marv, Dad, Uncle Pete, and so on) who continue to guide and help me get this work right. Thank you divine universe for your unending perfection!! And please forgive me for those times when I forget that everything is on purpose and that my intuition always gets me exactly and perfectly where I need to go.

WARNING

Everything you've heard from the media, advertisements, dating services, and your friends about finding true love is probably wrong. You won't find that advice here.

This book will help you remember who YOU are, what you signed up for, and how to find the partner you made a true-love agreement with before this life began.

PREFACE

LOVE IS THE ENERGY we swim in, the fabric of our divine universe, and the essence of our DNA. Yet today you may find yourself feeling alone, unloved, or afraid—lost in the struggle of your life.

How did this happen to you? When did you lose your connection to love and grace? Why are you alone when you came here to share your life with a soul mate?

Perhaps you've forgotten how this all began—that you came here on purpose to play in liquid love, bathe in the soup of divine energy, and manifest your sacred work. You knew the moment you were born that you were a superhero on a journey to change the world—with unlimited gifts to help you get it done.

You've experienced pain and loneliness when you've forgotten that mission—like an explorer who gets lost in the jungle without a map. Yet the sacred map is still inside of you. I'll teach you to access that map and find your way.

Let's step back and take a good look at you. Put down the burdens you're carrying. Take the heavy load off your back. Shake off the pain and disappointments that weigh you down. Cry if you need to. Just let it go . . .

True love IS waiting—but you have to reclaim YOU to find it.

Don't worry; you are not facing an impossible task. I recognize where you've been and the challenges you've faced. I see pain in your eyes and hear the fear in your voice. I feel your loneliness—but I also see your amazing beauty, your limitless power, your astounding genius, and the great work you came to share with the world. It takes my breath away.

In this book, I'll teach you to see this greatness in yourself and to embrace the person you came here to be. When you're back on path, your soul mate will stand beside you, fulfilling the agreement you made long before this lifetime began.

Yes, I see your soul mate—standing just behind you—waiting in the wings for you to remember your mission.

Heartbreak and loneliness occur NOT because of what anyone else has done to you, not because you're unattractive, and not because there aren't enough single people your age. You're not flawed, unlovable, or unlucky in love. A random tragedy did not ruin your life. No one unjustly stole your love away. There are no outside circumstances keeping you from finding true love. Only YOU stand in your way.

You ARE here on purpose to accomplish a powerful mission! You intended to be a fierce genius using your boundless gifts in your work—changing this world for the better.

You made agreements with all the important players in your drama before you got here—even in those relationships that have wounded you. Those agreements occurred to serve your highest good—to help you find your way.

This loneliness and pain is a tiny moment in the vast journey of your soul. It's your wake-up call. It's nudging you to turn your life in a powerful new direction and reclaim your soul power.

Perhaps your zealous grip on mundane reality has blocked your intuition. Our world's negative viewpoint may have sucked the life force from you.

Quit focusing on your flaws, and focus instead on your gifts and what you came to offer! Stop talking about what's wrong with the world, and ask how you can help raise the consciousness of the planet with your talents and wisdom.

Turn out the lights, unplug the TV, take down the mirrors, and take a long look at yourself. You may be attractive, sexy, fun, and smart, but what hides beneath?

Are you anything like the sweet, openhearted, loving soul you were when you started this journey? It's time to reclaim that divine essence, your true loving nature, and become who you came here to be—the hero of your story.

This book will take you down the path of powerful soul reinvention. At the end of this process awaits true love . . .

INTRODUCTION:
WHY ARE YOU ALONE?

It's not for the reason you think.

T'S A HUMBLING THING, heartbreak. When the whole world appears to be living in perfect love and happiness, your private pain weighs you down and sucks your breath away—keeping you from dancing at the party or taking another step forward. Instead, you get a headache and leave early, or drink the pain to sleep.

In my life, heartbreak came first as a young hippie-love boyfriend moving out, then as a husband dying in my arms, and then as another husband moving on—until I saw the problem. The problem was me not being ME.

Yes, it's true that my path is unusual and the work I came to do is odd, but that's what I chose for this lifetime—or at least it's the mission I accepted.

Yet when I got here, I wanted to be like everyone else—attractive, funny, smart, and successful, not spiritual, intuitive, or a teacher of sacred knowledge. Who knew?

Along the way, I chose men who were bright, charming, funny, and sexy—not spiritual. I dreamt of a sweet home with white wicker chairs where I would sit with my husband sipping iced tea and watching our children play. But that wasn't my agreement.

When I thought I'd finally found my man, my true love, he turned out to be my greatest spiritual teacher—dying in my arms instead of standing beside me to raise the children we dreamt of having.

I fell off the edges of the world then, widowed when others my age were having babies, disconnected from a normal thirtysomething life.

Everywhere I looked there were young healthy families, weddings, and baby showers. Yet my romances went nowhere, and I locked my spiritual insights and powerful intuitions away in angry silence.

In the years following my husband Paul's death from colon cancer, two more friends in their early thirties died from cancer. Grief became an ocean of pain that I tried to bury beneath exercise, work, and men.

I didn't want to hear that Paul's death was "for my highest good" or that "everything is on purpose." Instead, I focused on becoming a health journalist—teaching people to live healthy lives. If I could write one article that saved a person from cancer, I thought, perhaps my grief would slip away.

Yet, in my heart, I was connected more to the other realms where my loved ones had gone than this one. By the age of thirty-two, I perched on the edges of two worlds, not sure which one to claim. Too many people I dearly loved had died, leaving me to make sense of their suffering.

Repeatedly I asked myself, Why would sweet young people full of ambition and dreams die such painful deaths? And why was I chosen to stand beside them to help and then be left behind? Why was I still here?

Nightmares woke me up nearly every night. I dreamt I was trapped in a hospital, moving through rooms filled with suffering, sick, and terribly injured people—all calling for help. I would try to help one and then another, but I couldn't do anything to relieve their pain. When I tried to leave, each door I opened led to a new room of horrible suffering and screaming. I would wake in a panic.

I couldn't keep my food down. Images of Paul's outrageous physical suffering still lived vividly in my mind. His year of sickness had scarred me so badly I didn't know who I was anymore. I was hoping a man would save me—wrap me in love so passionate and profound that it would protect me from the ghosts at the edges of the room. But no one did—fortunately—or I would not be here doing my true work today. Heartbreak after heartbreak finally brought me back to ME.

As I embraced my strange, unconventional, intuitive gifts; my unlovable, different self; my unusual spiritual insights, I found my true work. And standing in the hallway to greet me then was my loving soul mate, Gene.

Today Gene and I have two life-affirming, happy, healthy children. The work I do is my passion and joy. It's the life I've always wanted. I didn't know it would require such a journey. I didn't know it would require me to own intuition and spiritual wisdom boldly as my work in the world.

Along the way, I've learned that we all come here on purpose, and that often the greater the mission we've signed up for, the greater the nudges to help us find our way. Those nudges can be quite painful—though they don't have to be. But when we ignore our intuition, pain seems to be the one thing that truly gets our attention here on planet Earth.

I've also learned that heartbreak is the most powerful fuel we can use to find our soul's true mission. A broken heart hurts so good that it makes us look beyond the surface and ask hard questions. It strips everything else away to help us remember our gift.

As a career intuitive and the author of *I See Your Dream Job*, I've shared intuitive and spiritual insights with others for more than ten years, helping thousands of clients, training hundreds of intuitive coaches, and teaching workshops across the country.

All of my clients struggle with relationships when they've lost their way. Yet once they embrace their true work, remember who they are and why they're here, their true path always brings them to love.

It's a popular misconception that we incarnate into human lifetimes looking for the soul mate who will give our lives meaning and purpose. We've got it backward. We each come here to do something great, to live up to our unique potential, and to help raise the consciousness of the planet. We ALL have a divine mission.

Our true partner stands in the wings—waiting for us to take responsibility for our journey, to step into the path of our true mission, and to remember who we are. Only then is our true love allowed to join us on our powerful path as a soul fulfilling its highest grace.

Some of us get to this great work sooner than others do. Some never get to it in a lifetime—but we all have opportunity after opportunity to get it right.

Along the way, we bump into many soul mates who nudge us in the right direction. Our true love waits at the end of the rainbow—our pot of gold for making the journey down the yellow brick road—moving beyond fear and pain to find our way back home.

PART

I

USING INTUITION
TO RECOGNIZE
YOUR SOUL MATE IN
A SEA OF FROGS

1

RECOGNITION UNDER A STREETLIGHT

We know everything we need to know. This knowingness speaks to us through our gut feelings, hunches, impressions, and perceptions. Yet we constantly talk ourselves out of this flawless inner wisdom.

When we fall in love (or meet someone new), we know instantly what the relationship holds in store for us. We remember our soul agreement. Yet we most often ignore it. Here's an example from my life: I intuitively knew the exact nature of my relationship with my now-departed husband, Paul, when I first met him.

Recognition . . .

After a long, delicious, rock-climbing day in the summer of 1978, our muscles aching from the dizzying walls of Eldorado Canyon, my friend Joel and I are feeling happy and tired. We're hungry and looking for a place to eat in town.

As we walk, we see a tall thin man approaching and waving. He knows Joel and we gather on the sidewalk to talk.

As Paul, my future husband, stands under a streetlight in the evening heat telling us about his bike ride, light shimmers around his head, creating a halo. He looks like an angel to me. I'm terrified and drawn to him at once. I know him before he says a word.

When he does speak, my world rips open into powerful soul-shaking recognition. I remember him. I feel devastating love, laughter, bliss, and loss—all at once.

As I extend my hand in greeting, I know that somehow this relationship will change me, break me apart. But the light emanating from Paul tells me that he's my greatest teacher and I need to take the journey.

After that meeting, it takes several months for our first date to manifest—both of us knowing in the deep pools of our intuition that this was a major shift, that a cosmic crack in our worlds is about to unfold.

It takes a while to move from joyful first embrace to the stunning cancer diagnosis that left him with only two weeks left to live to holding his frail body in my arms as his spirit slipped away. Yet the journey that Paul takes me on teaches me everything I need to know about my soul mission—who I am and why I've dropped into this physical realm. (Although that wasn't the lesson I wanted to learn at the time.)

Together we become spiritual travelers. We visit shamans, Native American healers who carry him to the other realms, as well as priests, therapists, nutritionists, herbalists, energy workers, and conventional cancer docs who love us passionately and weep with us at the end.

We spend too much time in hospital rooms enduring sci-fi procedures that suck our souls dry. When the room is filled with doctors, Paul's mother's fervent praying, endless tubes and drugs, we slide between the sheets deep into our comas—blissful, dream-filled travels to a parallel world of giggling babies and white picket fences. He builds me a house in his delirium, asking me to bring the hammer. He wants it to be solid, he says, eyes closed, pointing to the hospital room wall in front of us.

On the last day, I'll rage, protest, and refuse to give him back to the angels who gather around the bed. And in that final moment of his crossing, he'll show me his spirit with such clarity that it forever takes my doubt away.

Yet on that innocent, warm, happy evening of sweet dreams and sexy hope, in that one moment of meeting Paul under the street lamp, I felt the love, loss, joy, and grief all at once.

Today, fueled by the pain and wisdom of that shared journey, along with the unique gifts I brought into this lifetime, I've created the work that I love passionately and am successful at. As an intuitive, I see people's great potential, what they came here to do, who they came here to be, and what their challenges are in this lifetime.

I've been intuitive since my childhood in New Orleans, inheriting my Creole mother's telepathy and clairvoyance, but I didn't understand this powerful gift until long after Paul's death. I spent years never quite knowing what the visions meant, what to do with the dreams that came true down to the last detail, or how to decipher and share the powerful images and feelings I got when I spoke to people.

Falling in love has always opened wide my intuitive senses. Love has taught me that the heart rules intuition. We must open the heart to feel the truth of anything or anyone. To find your true work or your true love, your heart must be wide open, vulnerable, and fearless.

2

WHAT IS INTUITION?

"The intuitive mind is a sacred gift and the rational mind is a faithful servant. We have created a society that honors the servant and has forgotten the gift."

—ALBERT EINSTEIN

NTUITION IS YOUR GUT feeling. It is, above all else, a feeling from the heart. It marinates you in confidence, wisdom, and empowerment—never in fear. It's the connection to your true self, your raw, unrefined truth unclouded by the monkey mind. It's the shimmer of a spirit in the corner when you turn your head and the dream that wakes you up and stays with you. It's the knowingness that comes when you stop talking. It's the feeling that overpowers you in spite of logic. It's the voice whispering in your ear, and the nudge you often ignore in deference to being practical. It's our right-brain, expanded consciousness guiding our journey as planned.

Your intuition is your sacred pool of divine knowing. It's a gateway to your higher self. It's not linear, logical, or realistic. It's your dreamy, gut-feeling creativity—the part of you that knows the truth but doesn't know why it's true. Your intuition is your sweet spot. Robert Graves, an English poet, scholar, and novelist, said, "Intuition is the supra-logic that cuts out all the routine processes of thought and leaps straight from the problem to the answer."

Intuition can navigate you successfully toward finding true love as effortlessly as a dream in the night. It works better than dating sites, speed dating, or singles' events. Love is the gateway to your intuition.

You'll never be as intuitive as when you fall in love. Your energy centers are most open and receptive, and your monkey mind quiets down. You look into a stranger's eyes and remember him from another time. You know when he'll call. You feel his embrace long before it actually happens. And you sense what he's feeling even when the two of you are apart.

We're all a little more comfortable with intuitive loving than we are with intuitive living—using intuition for our everyday life and career choices. Yet we can tap into this portal of sacred guidance whenever we open our hearts. When you fall in love, nurture this sacred gateway to the unknown. When you're not in love, love anyway. It will open the door to your divine intuition and your highest self.

ARE WE ALL INTUITIVE?

Yes, we ARE all intuitive. We're all naturally able to access our right-brain hemisphere—the doorway to our intuition, creativity, and divinity. We talk ourselves out of listening to this inner guidance by focusing on our left-brain chatter—our linear-thinking, practical, realistic mind. We see logical thinking touted on the news, at work, and among our family members as "the truth, the whole truth, and nothing but the truth." Yet our left-brain logic is only telling us half of the truth. This supreme logic we live by has gotten us exactly where we are today—afraid, disconnected, unfulfilled, unhappy, and in search of meaning.

Being practical above all else does not get us where we want to go. It doesn't lead to a happy, fulfilled life. Our left-brain logic talks us out of being who we really are and doing the work we came here to do. And it sometimes talks us out of loving who we came here to love.

Remember, you are NOT your thoughts. You're an energy being, a pulsing wave of light connected to the energetic fabric that makes up the entire universe. Quantum physicists refer to this phenomenon as the membrane theory. When they say that we're all made of the same energy—waves of light that join everything and everyone—they're describing intuition! Your consciousness is so much bigger than your mind. Your feelings and intuition connect you to all other beings in our universe. Your intuition is a gateway to all the knowledge, answers, and guidance you've ever wanted.

When you're afraid, you block your intuition. Fear is the opposite of love, and fear shuts your portal to the divine. When you're tapped into fear you're hooked into low-vibration negative energy—or what I call pitiful thinking. This type of thinking makes your body feel bad; it drains your energy and makes you anxious. It clouds your connection to your higher self.

Intuition and divine guidance speak up in the quiet moments when your fear and mental chatter pause and you simply know what's true—you know it in your bones. It's a peaceful knowing brought to you courtesy of your highest self.

Our intuition announces exactly what we need to know exactly when we need to know it to fulfill our mission. Its timing is always perfect. And it uses any means available to reach us. You have the dream when you need the dream. You feel a strong urge to do something exactly when it's time to do it. You get a visual image of something you need to know while you're waiting at a stoplight. And you know you've met your soul mate the moment you hear his voice.

HOW DO YOU KNOW IF IT'S INTUITION?

How do you know your monkey mind isn't playing tricks? The answer lies in this question: how does the information make you feel when you receive it?

Intuition comes from the angels. It's not dark or scary—even when it's warning you about an upcoming crisis. It comes in a frequency of light and love. It makes you feel wise, compassionate, and empowered by knowledge. It shines light on your confusion and fear. It's the voice of the divine within you, and divine order is always on your side.

Pay attention to the gut feelings that make you feel excited, joyful, compassionate, empowered, and loving. Those are your intuitive thoughts. Whatever fills you with love and joy is right for you. Dismiss whatever fills you with fear and dread.

Mothers and their children have a natural intuitive connection because they're connected by a raw potent cellular love for one another. Here's an example of the mother-daughter intuitive connection:

One afternoon when my daughter was about eight years old, I got a call from her school. "Sarah fell in the gym, and we think she might have a concussion. Please come get her right away."

Every mom fears that kind of call. It instantly sent fear waves through my stomach. "On my way," I said jumping into the car. As I drove through traffic, I asked God to guide me and help me through this crisis.

While waiting at a red light, I instantly saw a vision of my daughter Sarah vomiting. I saw it vividly twice. Yet the overwhelming feeling that surrounded the vision was that everything would be OK. I felt calm, even though I saw her distraught and throwing up.

When I arrived at the school, Sarah ran up to me crying and said she had just thrown up twice. The teacher whispered that it was a sign of concussion and I needed to get Sarah to the hospital right away. We were only five minutes from the emergency room, but I made the drive in two. Yet underneath my stress and urgency was the powerful knowledge that came from the vision and my intuition— that she would be fine.

We spent nearly ten hours at the hospital, where Sarah had a CAT scan and underwent numerous tests and hours of observation. She did indeed have a mild concussion, and she felt sick most of the day. Yet by the time I got her home, we knew she was out of danger.

Overall, I was able to handle a scary day without getting lost in fear, thanks to the powerful intuitive guidance I received on the way to Sarah's school. That guidance allowed me to know that the problem was serious and that Sarah was in great pain and discomfort, but that she would be OK. I saw her throwing up at the exact moments she was sick. I'm still astounded by the perfect timing and detail of the intuitive guidance I received that day.

TRUSTING WHAT YOU GET

How often have you ignored a hunch? Dismissed an intuitive feeling or a precognitive dream? Each time you ignore your inner knowing, you weaken its voice within you. Your intuition is like a muscle: The more you use it, the stronger it gets. The less you use it, the weaker it gets.

If you ask for divine guidance and are given a sign or a gut feeling, pay attention to it! Our guides get frustrated when we constantly ignore them. They'll decide we're not an open channel for guidance and find someone else who is willing to listen.

When I first started working as a career coach in the 1970s, I got intuitive hunches and visions about my clients. I saw them involved in careers other than the ones they were currently pursuing. I had dreams about them and knew their life stories before I worked with them. But because I wasn't comfortable owning my gift, I would ignore my intuitive guidance and function as a conventional career coach, asking my clients questions and making them fill out endless sheets of information.

Once I began honoring my intuitive insights and immediately sharing them with clients, my intuition became more and more powerful. I learned to prepare for my clients' sessions by meditating on their paths to see their journeys, feel their gifts and talents, and download guidance designed especially for them.

Today, this intuitive insight helps my clients and students tremendously. Whenever a certain feeling or image pops into my field, I share it. Over the years, I've found that the most seemingly illogical tidbit of information that I receive for clients is often the most helpful. I've learned to trust what I get.

Today, I follow those hunches in every session and while making every decision in my own life—from where to have dinner to when to start a new book or what outfit to wear.

Several years ago, I spent a week in England visiting my daughter while she was studying at Oxford. I was by myself and had free time on my hands, so I bought a rail pass. From my base in Oxford, I decided to visit as many places in England as possible—guided by intuition.

Each morning, I intuitively decided where I would visit by meditating and picturing various cities and choosing the one that felt right. Once I arrived in a city, I continued to trust my gut. Each time I followed a certain street, took a particular turn, or stopped into a certain restaurant that felt right, my intuition rewarded me with a wonderful experience. From fabulous meals to meant-to-be conversations to once-in-a-lifetime opportunities and amazing new friends, my entire trip was an extraordinary experience. I even followed my intuition when waiting for buses (Did I miss that bus or not? Pause . . . Listen to the inner voice. Notice that feeling in my gut.

OK, keep waiting for the bus.) My intuition was ALWAYS right. By following my intuitive travel sense, I created a magical and divinely guided trip.

My favorite part was the day I spent in Liverpool. A lifelong Beatles fan, I arrived in Liverpool without reservations for the famed "History of The Beatles" guided bus tour. During that extraordinary day of following my intuition, I received a free ticket to the sold-out Beatles tour, got a free sack lunch for the trip, and struck up a friendship with Yoko Ono's hand-appointed guardian for John Lennon's childhood home. It was one of the most amazing days of my life.

This unplanned, intuitively guided England adventure was the most enjoyable vacation I've ever taken. On the flight home, I made a decision that I would never again dismiss my gut feeling—even over the smallest details. I would completely trust my divine guidance in every area of life. My guides have since rewarded me a hundredfold with stronger and stronger guidance.

3

HOW DOES INTUITION WORK?

E ACH OF US IS born with a left-brain hemisphere that allows us to organize information, master language, and learn to read. This left brain embodies the masculine energy of the linear, logical thought process.

We also arrive with a right-brain hemisphere, our gateway to intuition and expanded consciousness. Our right-brain hemisphere embodies the female energy of intuition, spirituality, and creativity. We sometimes call our right brain our authentic, spiritual, or intuitive self. Artists call it the doorway to creative inspiration.

Throughout our lives, we struggle to balance these two sides of ourselves. However, modern culture pressures us to favor left-brain logic over right-brain expanded consciousness. Modern neuroscientists describe our left mind as linguistic, organizational, sequential, methodical, rational, and smart—all highly valued qualities in our culture. On the other hand, these same scientists label the right mind as unpredictable, illogical, irrational, and potentially violent or insane. Even when we have a powerful intuitive spiritual self, we seldom pay homage to that on a résumé or tout it in a sales meeting. And it's usually NOT what we bring to the dinner table on a first date (even though it should be).

But to function well in this world we need easy access to both sides of the brain. Getting stuck in our left brain creates a spiritual crisis because life can seem meaningless and tedious. We can feel disconnected and doubt any reality beyond what we can see and touch.

Getting stuck in our right mind can make us scattered, impractical, ungrounded, dysfunctional, and sometimes emotionally disturbed. Or we can become a mystic—like Saint Francis of Assisi, who gave away his belongings and wandered in nature spreading the word of God. (He was my childhood hero. I thought he had the perfect career!)

Since our culture so highly values the left mind and its linear, logical processes, we learn early on in childhood that this is the important piece of the brain to develop—starting with words and language. We're slowly trained by teachers and loving parents to dismiss the right-brain impressions, visions, intuitions, and dreams—unless we're in an art class or attending an alternative school that emphasizes creativity and spirituality. As a result, many of us have lost our way. We've given such priority to our mental linear, logical chatter that we've completely silenced our right hemisphere's expanded perception of the world, including our intuition.

We have two minds for a reason: to use them both! We're designed to navigate this physical world (to build its roads and learn its languages) with our left mind, while we activate our higher purpose and artistic, spiritual, and intuitive gifts with our right mind, thus creating meaningful lives.

The purpose of human evolution, as I see it, is to merge these two viewpoints into one sustaining perspective that changes the way we live here on planet Earth. It's the shift of consciousness we're waiting for. It's the next step of our shared journey.

We can learn a lot about these dueling hemispheres from reading Dr. Jill Bolte Taylor's description of surviving a brain stroke that forever changed her perception of life. Before the morning of her stroke, at age thirty-seven, Taylor was a well-respected, published neuroanatomist performing and teaching brain research at Harvard Medical School.

On the morning of her stroke, as her left mind melted down, she observed the process just as any good scientist would. She noted her emerging right-brain consciousness and the profound spiritual insights she was gaining even as she was losing her ability to speak and dial a phone number to call for help. In her bestselling book, *My Stroke of Insight,* Taylor vividly describes this profound shift of awareness from fearful left-brain logic to blissful right-brain enlightenment.

Today, fully rehabilitated, Taylor speaks at medical conferences, making the case that our lives are out of balance because we're dominated by our left-brain perceptions and unaware of our intuitive, spiritual, right-brain consciousness. Taylor argues that we're missing half of the picture of who we really are, and it's the most important half.

THE SCIENCE OF INTUITION

Throughout my life, I've met many people who dismiss intuition as woo-woo. They claim that intuition hasn't been scientifically proved and shouldn't be taken seriously.

Yet people who so easily dismiss intuition are unaware of the work of several scientists, including Dean Radin, PhD, laboratory director at the Institute of Noetic Sciences and author of *The Conscious Universe* and *Entangled Minds.* Radin is the father of the modern study of psychic phenomenon and brings legitimate scientific rigor to intuition research.

Today, thanks to Radin's work, there are more than two hundred published scientific studies validating intuition in mainstream journals such as *Science, Psyche, British Journal of Psychology, Journal of Social Psychology, Journal of the American Society for Psychical Research, Journal of Parapsychology,* and the *American Journal of Psychology.*

For nearly two decades, Radin has conducted psychic research in academia, including at Princeton University, University of Edinburgh, University of Nevada, and in three Silicon Valley think tanks, including SRI International. For many years he worked as a scientist on a highly classified program investigating psychic phenomena for the U.S. government (loosely and humorously documented in the movie *Men Who Stare at Goats*).

Radin's long career explores the link between psychic phenomena and entanglement theory as described in quantum physics. His research shows how our thoughts and feelings are accessible to everyone through the quantum field. Entanglement, a prediction of quantum theory that Einstein couldn't quite believe (calling it "spooky action at a distance"), refers to the connections between separated particles that persist regardless of distance.

Radin believes that entanglement theory leads to a vastly improved understanding of psychic phenomena such as telepathy, clairvoyance, and precognition. The accumulated research, says Radin, clearly implies that "at very deep levels, the separations that we see between ordinary, isolated objects are, in a sense, illusions created by our limited perceptions. The bottom line is that physical reality is connected in ways we're just beginning to understand."

In laboratory studies (referenced in his bestselling book *Entangled Minds*), Radin cites overwhelming evidence of our ability to hear each other's thoughts and predict the future. He concludes that this repeatable laboratory evidence suggests that we have the capacity to perceive distant information and to influence distant events across space and time.

One of Radin's most fascinating studies, reported in the *Journal of Consciousness Studies,* suggests that people can affect others at a distance simply by thinking about them. His double-blind, controlled research measured physiological responses such as increased heart rate and respiratory functions among subjects who were "thought about" without their knowledge.

Researchers introduced the study participants to each other before the experiment began and then separated them in isolated, soundproofed rooms. At random times, the researchers asked subject A to think a thought about subject B, who was wired with electrodes to measure physiological responses. Repeatedly, subject B's physiological responses to being thought about showed measurable increases in heart rate and respiration at the exact moment when subject A focused attention on him or her.

Other examples of this fascinating research include a study in the journal *Foundations of Physics* in 2002 where the physicists Atmanspacher, Romer, and Walach explored how psychotherapists "know" things about their clients without being told. They concluded that entanglement theory operates in the world of psychotherapy as well and predicts "entangled mental states" between therapists and their clients.

These quantum connections describe the entanglement we all experience with our partners when we fall in love. We know when they'll call and we sense their embrace before it happens. This research also explains my ability to see my clients' life journeys, feel their pain, and understand their gifts even before I do a session with them.

TODAY . . .

My friend Marv sat on my shoulder today telling me to freshen up a chapter I was writing. He passed away several months ago, but his voice in my ear was strong and clear. "Just freshen it up," he whispered. So I did. Then he was gone. I can still see the golden cord connecting us through our many lifetimes of friendship.

Let me assure you that seeing into the other realms is the only thing I'm really good at here. It's the only career I could ever succeed at. And yet, when I first hit the dirt of planet Earth, I sprang into survival mode—forgetting everything I knew inside. I ignored the spirits in the room, dismissed my intuitive feelings, analyzed my precognitive dreams rather than accepting them for the gift they were. I learned to fit in. I wanted to be loved.

Most of us do forget everything when we land here. We look around at the limiting beliefs, the small-minded choices, the mind-less chatter, and we think, Oh, so this is how it's done here. And we begin the journey of forgetting ourselves, of disconnecting from our intuition.

If today you've lost your way and long to reconnect to your higher self, just know what you know. Speak beyond the illusion. Share a truth at the dinner table that shatters chatter and serves divinity as the main course.

Become the one voice in the crowd who shares wisdom when all other voices are small and afraid. Make this your calling. Use your higher self and divine intuition to recognize your soul mate and attract true love.

Do this once and the angels will pick you up where you stand and bring you into the realm of light. They'll smooth your clothes, wipe your face, and brush your hair. They'll sing the sweetest song you've ever heard. You'll remember it when you wake.

When you find yourself in the dirt once again, you'll know better and move to higher ground—using truth as your password to become the shaman on the hillside or the mystic at the dinner party. It's the only reason you came here.

4

QUIETING THE MIND TO RECEIVE INTUITIVE GUIDANCE

N OW THAT SCIENTISTS ARE validating our intuition, how do
    we learn to access it every day? How do we consistently quiet
our logical left minds enough to tap into our right brain's altered
consciousness?

The answer: through daily mantra-based meditation.

The greatest gift ever given to me was the practice of meditation. In my twenties, I experimented with meditation through
breathing exercises and yoga. But after my husband Paul died, I be-
friended a teacher of transcendental meditation (also known as TM)
who instructed me in the practice of mantra-based meditation.

This began my lifelong dedication to using mantra—or sacred
words and sounds—to quiet my mind. This type of meditation
works by giving the monkey mind something to chew on (a repeti-
tive sound) so that it's lulled into a quiet state. This allows access to
the right-brain consciousness that lies beyond our thoughts.

Since that first powerful lesson in TM, I've sat at the feet of numerous gurus, lived in and out of ashrams, and taken classes from
many great teachers, all of whom improved and added to my meditation practice. Today, daily meditation is the cornerstone of my life
and work. It's the gateway to my intuition.

Once again, numerous scientific studies have shown us the

value and validity of this type of meditation. For example, at the University of Wisconsin, researchers studied the brain activity of monks in meditation (comparing their activity to a control group of nonmeditators). The researchers discovered that during meditation, the monks were able to quiet all the random thought activity in their brains (as measured by electrodes) and sit perfectly still for long periods. The control group of nonmeditators couldn't control their thoughts or focus their minds and were unable to sit still for more than five minutes.

When I began my practice of daily mantra-based meditation, I learned the art of quieting the mind—a technique that greatly magnified my intuition. Meditation turned up the volume on my intuitive feelings and helped me remember more clearly my precognitive dreams. Within one month of daily mantra meditation, I was able to solve most day-to-day problems with a twenty-minute mind-clearing meditation. As a result, I became more successful at my journalism career and again later in my intuitive work with clients.

During the years I spent working as a magazine editor in my thirties, I made it a daily practice to close my office door from two to two thirty for meditation. When I emerged from these afternoon meditations, the rest of my day was definitely more productive and focused than when I skipped my meditation. In my current career, meditation is the tool I use daily to enhance intuition and tap into divine guidance.

Meditation has numerous other benefits besides clearing the mind and enhancing intuition. The American Medical Association's *Archives of Internal Medicine* recently published a study showing that mantra-based meditation is highly effective in preventing high blood pressure, diabetes, and obesity.

A symposium hosted in March 2006 by the American College of Cardiology touted research conducted at more than a dozen independent universities on the positive effects of mantra-based meditation

for reducing heart disease, hypertension, stroke, cholesterol, atherosclerosis, and heart failure.

These studies have repeatedly found positive correlations between daily meditation and reduced blood pressure, improved quality
of life, metabolic regulation, reduced atherosclerosis, decreased risk of
heart disease, reduced anxiety levels, and enhanced psychological indicators, including self-understanding and self-awareness.

MEDITATING TO ENHANCE INTUITION

Sit comfortably without letting your head lean back against anything (a sure way to fall asleep). Close your eyes and take several
deep, releasing breaths.

Silently repeat either *Om Namah Shivaya* or the Lord's Prayer or
another sacred sound of your choice. Sit for ten minutes (at least) silently repeating these words. When you notice your mind paying
attention to thoughts, gently bring your focus back to mantra or
prayer. Don't struggle. Be gentle.

After ten minutes, slowly stop repeating the words. In this quiet
gap before getting up and going back to your routine, ask for guidance. Say, "Show me my next step for fulfilling my highest good." Or,
"Show me my next step for preparing for my soul mate." Or, "Show
me my next step for loving my soul mate."

5

DREAMING ABOUT
YOUR SOUL MATE

N THE 1900 EDITION of Sigmund Freud's book *Interpretation of Dreams,* the father of modern psychology wrote about his own dreams and his interpretation of them. One of those documented dreams clearly foretells his future illness and eventual death from mouth cancer twenty-eight years later.

His documented dream even offers a solution—stop smoking cigars—but Freud interprets this dream in his own narrow parameters of sexual metaphors. He fails to see the divine gift of premonition and solution that the dream offered.

Freud's approach gives us a great example of left-brain logic dismissing right-brain intuitive guidance. Are you doing something similar with your dreams? Do you dismiss your inner guidance by analyzing dreams only from a psychologist's perspective? Or you do you ignore your dreams completely?

Perhaps you believe that you don't dream at all. Of course you do! You're simply allowing left-brain logic to step in immediately when you awake and erase your dream memories. Before going to sleep, sit up in your bed and do a short meditation. At the end of the meditation, ask your guides for dream guidance. Keep a notebook by your bed. The moment you wake up, write down any dream memories you can capture.

My dreams have been one of my primary tools for seeing the future and understanding my clients' journeys. These dreams began when I was very young. I would announce at the breakfast table that my aunt Ruby was going to visit us that day or that my cousin had gotten sick during the night. These dreams would be validated when Aunt Ruby showed up unannounced or we got the phone call that Cousin Russell had the chicken pox. In elementary school, I learned quickly that sharing these dreams only got me bullied on the playground or in trouble with the nuns. So I kept them to myself.

When I was in high school, my precognitive dreams became so intense that I had to share them with someone I trusted. I chose my father. After he witnessed a few of my dreams come true down to the last detail, he became fascinated in an engineer's way with wanting to understand how precognition worked.

One morning, I told my dad about a dream in which I was coming home from school on Old Shell Road in my friend Gwen's car (but Denise was driving). A large green truck with two green doors and a silver padlock holding them shut was right in front of us. It braked suddenly, and our car slammed into it.

As I told my father about this dream on the way to school, we argued about whether people dreamt in color. In the 1960s, people believed that dreams were only in black-and-white. I insisted that the truck was green.

By the end of the school day, I had forgotten the dream. Gwen offered me a ride home, and we headed down Old Shell Road. After a few minutes of driving, Gwen said she had a headache, and we pulled over to let Denise drive.

We were laughing about an upcoming school dance, when the green truck with two doors held together by a silver padlock pulled in front of us.

"It's my dream!" I screamed. "Don't hit it!" Denise slammed on the brakes just as the truck suddenly slammed on its brakes in front

We each come here on a specific path that's revealed in the numbers of our date of birth. This birth path number reveals what we've come here to do as well as the gifts and challenges we came to experience. In the following stories, I refer to these birth path numbers. If you want to skip ahead to chapter 9, this is where you can determine your own path number and what it reveals.

of us. We barely avoided the collision. No one was hurt, but from that moment I began to consider that my dreams could have a purpose.

Today I dream about my partners, family members, and clients almost every night. Here's one example:

IN A DREAM . . .

In my dream, my husband is betraying me—even though he is someone I've never met in real life. He's tall, blond, young, and charismatic and I love him dearly. We have two small children and live in a spacious suburban house. One day, he brings home a young blond woman. The two are madly in love. Holding her and kissing her, he brings her into our bedroom to show me.

At first, I'm angry and try to be manipulative and controlling to get him to stop seeing her. When that doesn't work, I am devastated and hurt so badly that I wake up from the dream with my heart aching. I'm in tears when I wake up.

After going back to sleep, the dream continues. I beg my husband to give up the young girl and return to me. He refuses. When the pain is so bad I can't stand it anymore, I say, "I don't need you in my life. I'm happier without you." I turn away from him and start thinking about my own life. Supportive people who tell me what a powerful person I am suddenly surround me. They bring me out into the world for "work." I wake up feeling powerful, strong, happy with myself, and excited about my future.

In the morning, I'm stunned by the realizations that even though I knew none of the people in this dream, it lasted all night and the emotions I felt were so powerful that I actually woke up crying at one point and happy at another.

As I take the kids to school, I can't stop thinking about the dream and what it means. Later, I look at the path of my first client and see that she's a woman in her forties who has two young daughters and who is going through a divorce. I look at the path of her husband and quickly realize that he was the man in the dream who was betraying his wife with another woman. The dream must be for my client Helen.

The dream contains a message that I must share with Helen to help her find her power. I tell Gene about the dream. "Be careful," he says. "What if she doesn't know that her husband is cheating?"

But in the dream the man was very blatant about the cheating, flaunting the woman in front of me, bringing her into my home. "I'm sure she knows," I reply.

When the session begins, I explain to Helen that she is on the powerful birth path of the number 8, which means she's meant to be successfully working in the world of business finding and owning her power and learning to use it for good. I explain that even though she has already developed many other aspects of herself in other lifetimes, this time she is required to be a successful entrepreneur. I tell her that my guides said she was being kicked out into the world now to fulfill her lifetime mission and own her power.

Helen tells me that she's been a stay-at-home mom for years and has been unhappy. But now she's going through a divorce and will reinvent herself and get into the world of career. After we go into more detail about what that could look like, I say, "I had a dream, Helen, that I think pertains to you. Can I share it with you?"

"Sure. Don't candy-coat anything. Just tell it to me straight," she says. So I do—down to the last detail. She cries all during the telling of my dream. Then she tells me a story.

"A couple of months ago I discovered that my husband is addicted to Internet porn. We hadn't had sex in so long, and I felt so neglected. By sheer chance I stumbled upon the evidence of it on his computer. It was shocking stuff and it went on every night. And here's the thing. He was doing it in our bedroom on the computer after I went to sleep. He was bringing the young blonde into our bedroom through the computer.

"When I confronted him with it, he said that he had been doing it for years and was addicted. So at first, I thought we could fix it and we went to therapy. But now he's still living in the house with us, in a separate bedroom, and I've filed for divorce. But he won't move out. And he won't give up the porn. And I'm trying to be understanding with him so we can have an amicable divorce."

Helen cries as she tells me her story, and I wait for her to calm down before I begin: "Someone in the other realms really wants you to get him out of the house, so you can find your strength and power. It was very clear in my dream that as you turn away from him, you find your power in the world."

Helen's so grateful for the confirmation that what she feels about this situation is right. By the end of the session she feels confident about getting a lawyer and getting her husband out of the house while she gets her new career going. I tell her that her true soul mate will someday support her as her most powerful self and not demean her. But first she's required to take steps in the right direction before he's allowed to show up. She agrees that that feels right. Together we make a plan for Helen's new life as an entrepreneur.

FALLING IN LOVE WITH GENE . . .

Here's my story of dreaming about my husband Gene before I met him.

First, I fell in love with my work, helping others through my new career-coaching business. The work opened my heart and shifted my energy. I was a single mom, had survived a traumatic divorce, and had finally launched my true work. It was a major reinvention. I had discovered enlightened teachers and inspiring ideas that were shifting my frequency in a huge way. I felt happy!

Then I fell into an ocean of love with Gene; in my dream, he approached with wide-open arms, smelling of pepper and incense. I loved his scent and fell into his arms. I saw his wise and kind face. His voice was deep and powerful, "Honey," he whispered as he approached me with a tenderness that opened me up completely. I woke up. Who was that? I wondered. He was not someone I knew yet.

Months later, we met in person . . .

Early one morning after dropping my daughter off in her classroom, I walked into the hallway and bumped into another parent named Gene, a single dad dropping off his son, Kai.

He was powerful, dignified, and incredibly handsome. I'd seen him in the hallway before and felt a longing to have a man like that in my life. But I had my hands full being a single mom and running a new business. I wasn't ready.

I knew from what I'd heard around the school that Gene, Kai's dad, was a gifted designer and had run a successful design and marketing company for many years. He sounded wonderful, successful, and conventional. I was probably not his kind of girl. And I was certainly not beautiful enough for an artist. But he looked so kind and loving.

As he opened his mouth to speak to me, I remembered my dream. It was HIS face, HIS scent, HIS voice that I had dreamt of months earlier. Standing in the hallway face-to-face, I fell headfirst into his energy field and got lost in a world of passion, deep connection, fun, and true love. I heard it all in his powerful voice. I knew him already. My head filled with visions of us together. He talked about his son Kai, his difficult divorce, his ex-wife, and his design company. Then he asked about my daughter.

I struggled to find my voice. Meeting him had just opened my heart wide and filled my head with visions.

"She loves school most of the time," I answered. "Sometimes she wants to stay home with me though. We're very close. But I have to work."

"What do you do?"

"I'm a career coach," I whispered, still trying to find my voice among the swirling images of us together.

"That's awesome," he said. "You're helping people. So many folks are lost. How exactly do you help them? Do you use career tests?"

It was my decisive moment. Should I speak my truth, reveal who I really was, and watch him run? Should I mention the I word—"intuition"?

Something in my heart urged me to speak my truth. "I use my intuition to help people remember who they are. I explain their mission and help them line that up with career."

His eyes lit up with new interest. A warm smile spread across his handsome face. He truly looked at me for the first time.

I had just come through a 9 personal year of endings, divorce, and career reinvention. I was about ten pounds overweight. My life as a working single mom left little time to take care of myself. He seemed to see far beyond all of that.

Then he began talking about intuition, about how he used it to create graphic design for his clients. And right there, in the school hallway with parents and kids bustling by, we remembered each other.

"Do you need a Web site or business cards? Let me look at what you already have put together, and I'll give you some ideas for taking it to the next step," he offered as we parted.

And so our business-based friendship began. We exchanged e-mails and URLs. When I looked at his design work, I saw how extraordinary he was. And I began to trust him—as a friend.

We had several lunch meetings to discuss new Web site designs. I introduced him to friends and clients who owned businesses and needed his talents. We got very used to discussing business, design, and intuition together. It felt safe, fun, and easy.

We both had young children and felt guilty that our marriages had ended in divorce. We were each trying to make amends to our children by devoting all of our love and time to them. Being friends with each other was the best we could do.

Months went by. I moved into my 2 personal year, which on that cycle was an 11/2 personal year of inspiration and love.

One evening at a school fund-raising event, Gene and I ended up sitting across the table from one another. At one point in the evening several single moms were flirting with Gene and playfully sitting on his lap. But our eyes never left each other, gazing across the table—beyond the frenzy—lost in our soul connection.

It was a small crack in our very safe friendship, and it left me afraid that I would lose what we had created. At the same time, I didn't want anything to jeopardize my relationship with my daughter or my precarious life as a working single mom.

Another few weeks of friendly lunch meetings went by. Finally, Gene called and asked me to dinner on a Friday night. I wanted to know his intention, so I asked if it was a business meeting. "No, it's a date!" he replied firmly.

When the evening arrived, we were both nervous. He picked

me up at my house and we began driving to a nearby restaurant for dinner. As we talked and drove, we forgot our dinner plans and fell into an entangled state of deep, heartfelt connection, great fun, and shared laughter.

I don't remember a word we said, but I remember the joy and ease of it. I felt light pulsing between us. It felt like coming home, like talking to an old friend from long ago. We ended up driving forty miles into the mountains to Estes Park, where we eventually shared dinner and our first passionate kiss.

From that moment on, we've built our life together. Today, nearly ten years later, it's still the best relationship I've ever known. Gene is a gifted 7 path with powerful artistic and intuitive energy. We've merged our families more harmoniously than we ever expected. No one has ever embraced my intuition and spirituality the way Gene does. He's the person I go to for insight, laughter, passion, and encouragement. In turn, I deeply honor his gracious heart, loving nature, profound artistic talent, and powerful intuition.

HOW OUR DREAMS CAN HEAL US

Many times when I've been in pain, a departed loved one has come into my dreams to heal me. Here's my most powerful example:

I met my lifelong best girlfriend Crissie in second grade on the swing set of our Catholic elementary school playground. Her crazy brilliance and insane wit bonded us instantly. Our first conversation went something like this (although she was doing all the talking): "Don't you think the word 'nunnery' is weird, like a cannery? Why would a girl choose to be canned . . . er . . . nunned? Do you think nuns all come out the same from a nunnery like peas from a cannery? What if Shakespeare said, 'Get thee to a cannery'?" As she talked, she cracked herself up, bending over in peals of giggles that had me laughing uncontrollably along with her. I realized I had found a true friend—someone who thought outside the box. I didn't always understand her, but I loved her instantly.

Years later in seventh grade, The Beatles appeared on *Ed Sullivan*. Crissie and I were the only ones in our Catholic elementary school to have our lives changed at that moment. We knew The Beatles meant more than wonderful music and that they were showing us a bigger, more exciting life that we both wanted. We promised each other that we'd get out of the South as soon as we graduated high school and that we'd fulfill our huge dreams. She never let me forget that promise.

Her brilliance put her at the top of every class and got her accepted into Georgetown University in 1969 as one of a small group of the first women ever accepted to that prestigious college in Washington, D.C. When I told her I had been accepted into University of Missouri to study journalism, she forever called it University of Misery and told me I should have "aimed for a coast." (She was right! But I wasn't as smart as she was, so I was grateful for the chance to attend University of Misery.)

Our friendship lasted long beyond my stint at Misery and hers at Georgetown. Her first true love had been a fellow student at Georgetown University named Paul Frederick, whom she became engaged to. Two months before the big southern wedding her parents had happily planned, Paul Frederick dumped her. Crissie never truly got over it.

Later when I moved to Colorado and met a handsome mountaineer named Paul Frederick (not the same guy), I was immediately leery of him. Would he break my heart too? (Turns out he did.) Crissie was the first friend to come visit us. She liked him instantly.

When my Paul Frederick was diagnosed with cancer, Crissie's frequent phone calls helped me cope. With Crissie, every conversation was about exploring new ideas, asking tough questions, and searching for the truth—all done in a gleefully witty way. I adored her. She asked me the toughest questions anyone ever did. And she made me laugh harder than anyone I knew. She always told me I was a gifted writer and should "just write dammit!"

Six months after Paul died, Crissie came to visit. She cheered me up and challenged me simultaneously. What was I doing with my life now? Was I moving forward? Was I writing? She prodded and poked as we drove to the mountains to ski. She seemed healthy, energetic, lonely as usual, but generally happy with her California graduate student lifestyle. (She was getting a PhD in botany.)

On her flight back home to California, she noticed bruises appearing on her body. By the time she landed in San Francisco, she was covered in bruises and rushed by ambulance to the hospital. Her stunning leukemia diagnosis so soon after Paul's death was overwhelming. After this devastating news, I suffered several anxiety attacks where my throat would tighten up and I couldn't swallow or eat. I felt nauseated most of the time.

Crissie's mother moved to California to take care of her, and her father got her into the most advanced treatment of the time—a bone marrow transplant at Fred Hutchinson hospital in Seattle. Surrounded by friends and family, she went through chemo and radiation treatments and nearly died during the torturous bone marrow transplant. I couldn't understand why someone as bright, loving, and good as Crissie would have to go through such suffering—as horrible as Paul's experience. In deep despair and grief, I sold my belongings and moved to Mexico to teach fitness at a resort. I needed healing and was dropping out of a world that made no sense anymore.

When Crissie was finally in remission, she moved back to California and resumed graduate studies. But she was only thirty-one years old and had been through hell. She was in a deep spiritual crisis, wondering what the purpose of life was. I understood her pain.

We stayed in touch with letters and phone calls. She began getting her life going again and started to feel better. She yelled at me when I told her I was in love with a married (but separated) Mexican man named Emilio who ran the local dive shop. "Sue Ellen, you'll only get your heart broken! You're a writer so you can use it in something I guess . . . but really. Come back home and write dammit!" I couldn't come home yet. My peaceful life of snorkeling and diving every day with Emilio was a form of healing for me—even if I knew Emilio would never be my lifelong partner. I loved him anyway.

Crissie and I made a plan to see each other back on our childhood turf. Crissie flew to the Gulf Coast to visit her family at the same time I flew home to visit mine. Our dads both owned fishing boats and had beach houses. Crissie's dad brought her over to the harbor near our beach house to spend time with us. My dad (who loved Crissie) took us fishing and boating. When we got bored with fishing, he dropped us off at a remote island to talk while he fished around the island.

Crissie and I walked and talked for hours along the sandy shore and crystal clear water of our tiny remote island. We talked about her ongoing struggle with leukemia, her bone marrow transplant, her feelings about death, my grief over Paul, my attempts to end my ill-fated relationship with Emilio, and her heartbreaking belief that she would never find a soul mate or have children. She felt alone and unlovable. "What's the hardest part?" I asked her. "Disappointing my dad," she said as tears flowed. "He wants me to live so badly . . ." I knew then that she was dying, no matter what the doctors said. I recognized the process of letting go that she was experiencing. It was the same conversation I'd had with Paul.

When my dad picked us up on the island, he took us back to the marina, where Crissie's dad waited on his fishing boat. As our dads laughed and joked with each other, Crissie and I hugged one last time. She couldn't look me in the eye as she turned away and stepped onto her dad's boat. As their boat moved out of the harbor, Crissie and I waved. When she was out of view, I broke down in uncontrollable sobs. My dad gently asked, "Why are you so sad? She looks great. She's going to make it." I turned to him crying and said, "Dad, this is the last time I'll ever see her. I know it." Crissie returned to her home in California. I returned to Mexico. Three months later she was dead.

The night of her death, before I knew she had died, Crissie came to me in my dreams. We spent the entire night laughing and giggling together (the way she and I always did). When I woke up, my stomach muscles were actually sore from laughing so hard. I've never before or since experienced such physical sensations after a dream as I did from that night with Crissie.

That morning as I was making coffee and about to call the States and check in with Crissie, I got the phone call telling me she had died during the night. I realized she had visited me in my dreams to let me know she was fine and to tell me that death wasn't the end of anything.

But Crissie wasn't done teaching me yet. A year later, I was finally back living in the States, heartbroken over Emilio, and trying to get my life and career on track. My grief over the loss of Crissie, Paul, and Emilio was weighing me down with sadness and depression.

One night, Crissie came to me in a dream and healed my heartbreak. In the dream, Crissie and I are standing on a white stone balcony overlooking an emerald-green sea. It's peaceful and extraordinarily beautiful and I feel so content standing beside her. We're talking as we always did but not using words. She's standing a bit behind me and to my left as we look out over the water. I notice that her physical body is shimmering and seems to be more like dappled light than a fully formed physical presence. The form that I know as Crissie is changing. Her hand is on my back, rubbing it in circles while she talks to me. We're discussing my heartbreak over Emilio.

She pulls out several handwritten letters on many different pieces of stationery that Emilio had written to his estranged wife (who lived in another city during our relationship). In the letters Emilio is professing his undying love for his wife. Page after page contains stories of how well his diving business is going and how wonderful their life will be when he returns home to her. Crissie makes it clear to me that Emilio never really loved me and I have to let him go and move on. As she shows me these letters, my pain and grief from all of my losses well up in my chest. While she rubs my back, a loud, wailing cry escapes me; the sound soars across the emerald sea in front of us. It's powerful, ancient, and deep—louder than any sound I've ever made. As this pain pours out of me and flows across the water, Crissie lovingly rubs my back and encourages me to let it all go.

When I've finished crying, Crissie slowly disappears beside me. I wake up still hearing the sound of my painful wailing and feeling Crissie's hand on my back. I cry most of the morning. But as the days go by, I realize that my grief has subsided. Finally I'm able to begin a journey of reinvention and spiritual exploration that pushes me toward the work I do today.

6

WORKBOOK FOR DEVELOPING YOUR INTUITION

STEP ONE

REMEMBERING PAST INTUITIVE MOMENTS

Describe moments in your life when you've felt intuitive or had intuitive experiences:

_____

_____

_____

_____

Describe your most memorable precognitive or healing dream:

_____

_____

_____

_____

What did you learn from these experiences?

Were these experiences encouraged or dismissed by your family of origin?

Does your current circle of friends and partners embrace or dismiss intuition?

Do you remember feeling intuitively connected to your last partner when you fell in love? Describe this experience:

_____

_____

_____

_____

Who in your life now do you feel intuitively connected to? Describe how this manifests in your life:

_____

_____

_____

_____

Do you believe you can strengthen your intuitive abilities? List three steps you're willing to take to do this:

1. _____

2. _____

3. _____

Are you ready and willing to own your intuition, trust the guidance you receive, and speak your truth?

If not, what's holding you back? How can you change that?

STEP TWO

MEDITATING TO ENHANCE INTUITION

Sit comfortably without letting your head lean back against anything (a sure way to fall asleep). Close your eyes and take several deep, releasing breaths.

Silently repeat either *Om Namah Shivaya* or the Lord's Prayer or another sacred sound of your choice. Sit for ten minutes (at least) silently repeating these words. When you notice your mind paying attention to thoughts, gently bring your focus back to mantra or prayer. Don't struggle. Be gentle.

After ten minutes, slowly stop repeating the words. In this quiet gap before getting up and going back to your routine, ask for guidance. Say, "Show me my next step for fulfilling my highest good." Or, "Show me my next step for preparing for my soul mate." Or, "Show me my next step for loving my soul mate."

STEP THREE

INTUITIVE LIVING

Right now, test out a possible choice in your future to see how it feels in your body. This could be a small choice, such as what restaurant to go to, or a large choice, such as what career or lover to choose.

See yourself doing this as if it's already been decided and you're living in that future. See yourself sitting in the restaurant, eating its food. Notice everything around you. How does it feel? Or see this partner standing beside you five years from today. Do you feel happy beside him?

Check in with your physical body sensations. Are you smiling and feeling good in this possible future? That's a yes from your intuition. If you feel tired, drained, or fearful in your body, that's a no from your intuition.

Practice your intuition every day. Before heading home from work ask, "Should I take this route or the other route?" Now close your eyes and see yourself on one of the possible routes home and note how your body feels. Do you get a good or bad feeling in response to seeing that particular drive? If it's good, take that route home.

Afterward, reflect on how the commute went for you. Was it easier than usual? Was there less traffic?

Plan an intuitively guided vacation. Visit a new city and plan your activities each morning based on your gut feelings. Keep a journal of how this works for you.

As you learn to trust your intuition for these little everyday choices, you'll be better able to trust your intuition for the big life choices of love, career, and health.

EXTRA CREDIT: GETTING DREAM GUIDANCE

Before going to sleep, sit up in your bed and do a short meditation. At the end of the meditation, ask your guides for dream guidance. You can be specific and ask to meet your soul mate. Or you can ask for healing and comfort from a departed loved one. Keep a notebook by your bed. The moment you wake up, write down any dream memories you can capture.

STEP FOUR

INTUITIVE DATING

Before going on a first date (especially a blind date), write down your date's name and place your hand over it. Close your eyes and do a short meditation with mantra to quiet your mind.

Now ask to see what the person looks like and feel their energy. If the energy you feel and the person you see makes you smile and giggle, that's a yes from your intuition. Your higher self is telling you that this person will be a loving presence in your life.

If the energy feels bad in your stomach and makes you feel anxious, cancel the date. If the energy you feel revs up your sexual chakra, that's telling you what the focus of this relationship will be.

If you don't feel a loving, warm energy in your heart while picturing and feeling this person's energy, this probably won't be a long-lasting or fulfilling relationship.

EXTRA CREDIT

If you have the person's date of birth, decipher his birth path (as explained in chapter 9) and write his name and birth path on a sheet of paper. Put your hand on this information and meditate to quiet your mind. Now ask to feel the person's energy and understand his journey. Ask if this person is someone you should connect with for your highest good. Pay attention to the feeling you get and note whether it's positive or negative. Write down any thoughts about this person and birth path that come to you during your meditation.

If you're using dating Web sites, print out a potential date's photo, name, and information. Practice this intuitive meditation technique using her photo, name, and birth date (if it's available). Notice your gut reaction. How do they feel to you? Trust your gut. If it feels bad, don't pursue this person no matter how beautiful the photo or how brilliant her story.

(You'll notice that I am switching between male and female pronouns. It doesn't feel right to discuss these paths in either all-male or all-female terms. We've all been men and women interchangeably in many lifetimes, and we each experience the energies of these paths multiple times as men and women.)

Keep practicing. Use this intuitive technique with potential hires at your workplace or to decide whether to take a new job.

The more you use your intuition, the more you'll trust it. Eventually you'll realize how good you are at trusting your intuition.

You are now becoming a master of intuitive living, an approach that will put you right into the juicy flow of your life and bring you love, success, and happiness each day.

STEP FIVE

PROTECTING YOURSELF

Years ago, I was meditating on a client's birth path when a dark blob of negative energy dropped directly down onto my lap. It startled me so badly that I screamed and jumped up from my meditation. I quickly said the Lord's Prayer then chanted *Om Namah Shivaya* and burned incense in the room to cleanse the space. Finally, the dark energy cleared and I was able to finish my meditation on the client.

During the session, I learned that earlier in his life my client had been a drug dealer and was involved in a drug-related crime. He had since reformed his life. But that dark energy spirit was still following him around. During the session, we spent a lot of time talking to this spirit, sending it the energy of forgiveness, and asking it to leave my client alone and move forward to the next realm. We meditated and prayed over this until we both felt the spirit had left.

I share this story to stress the importance of understanding how intuition works and how you need to ground yourself in basic spiritual principles before dabbling in the other realms. When we connect to our expanded consciousness (or intuition), our spirits are traveling in the other dimensions. Just as there are positive energies in the universe, there also are negative ones. Our universe is composed of both light and dark, yin and yang. When we venture into the other realms, we need to wrap ourselves in high-vibration prayer, mantra, or chanting. This protects us from anything negative.

RECOMMENDED PROTECTION TECHNIQUES

The Lord's Prayer has been used in the Christian tradition for centuries to call in the light and protect us from dark energies. It's an extremely powerful high-vibration prayer. Repeat it whenever you feel afraid.

The mantra *Om Namah Shivaya* is a Sanskrit phrase meaning, "I bow to the divine self." This sacred, high-vibration chant has been used for thousands of years to raise consciousness and will also wrap you in protective energy. I use it every day in my meditations and before working with clients.

Energy healers often use techniques such as picturing a bubble of white or blue light surrounding and protecting them. I've also found this to be helpful.

In my years of studying Hinduism and Buddhism, I've used many spiritual cleansing techniques, but here is my favorite: Sit on the ground in meditation position with legs folded. Extend your arms straight down to the ground so that your fingertips touch the floor. Visualize running energy from the top of your head down through your fingertips and into the ground. This practice works to flush negativity and exhaustion from your body and send them into the earth to be recycled.

Water is a powerful cleansing agent and you can use it to do more than just cleanse your body. Swimming, showering, or taking a bath will also energetically cleanse you—washing away any dark or negative energies or feelings you've picked up during your day. Adding salt to your bathwater gives it more energy-cleansing power. If water isn't available, sit in meditation and picture a shower or waterfall pouring over your head and washing away everything negative from you until you feel pure and light.

Love is the most powerful positive force of all, and it always trumps darkness. Whenever you're afraid, this will help you: Sit in meditation until you can feel love for just one person in your life. See that person wrapped in your powerful love. Pump the love to this person until you see them smiling and laughing. Now extend that love energy out to the entire space around you, filling it with golden light. Now pump the love out to the entire world. See our planet wrapped in golden love and light, and all of its people looking peaceful and happy. Spend time with that image. When you open your eyes, the room you're sitting in will shimmer with love and light. Your fear will be gone.

STEP SIX

A FIVE-STEP TEST FOR RECOGNIZING YOUR TRUE SOUL MATE IN A SEA OF FROGS

If you've begun dating someone, it's helpful to try these techniques to help determine if he's right for you:

1. When you come home from an evening together, notice how you're feeling about yourself. Sit in quiet contemplation for five minutes. Take note of your energy. Are you happy and loved? Have you been laughing a lot during your date? Do you feel energized?

   If the answer to these questions is yes, this is a healthy relationship and will help you thrive in your life. If instead you feel tired, drained, depleted, unhappy, criticized, or unloved, it's a sign that it's not a good relationship and will only make you feel worse as time goes on (no matter how strong your physical attraction is).

2. Try my intuitive-living exercise: Sit in meditation and quiet your mind. Then move into your future five years from the present day. See your future life with this partner. Look at where you're living, how you communicate, what you're doing together, how you feel standing beside him in the future. Notice how your body feels in response to that future image. Do you feel excited, happy, energized? Are you smiling when you see it? Or do you feel drained, depleted, or anxious. Your body is telling you whether this relationship will have a positive or negative effect on your life.

3. Take the laughter test: Plan a silly date of meaningless activities like playing cards, miniature golf, or a child's board game such as Clue. Notice how often you laugh together and whether "doing nothing" feels easy or difficult. A positive relationship will feel joyous and filled with laughter even when you're doing silly, meaningless things together.

4. Get a notebook and ask your partner what gifts he sees in you. Write them down. Tell him the gifts you see in him. If he doesn't mention the core qualities and unique gifts you know about yourself, it's not a good sign. If he mentions those qualities and more, this is a good fit. Remem-

ber these qualities need to be much more than superficial traits like beauty and sexuality.

5. Pay close attention to the role of sexuality in your courtship. If most of your time together is spent focused on your sexual connection and not your friendship, this isn't good. Sexuality is one way to measure your chemistry and it's important. However, for a lifelong partnership, the communication, deep understanding, and shared laughter are the indicators of success. If more than half your time together is spent in communication, friendship, and laughter, this relationship is a winner.

EXTRA CREDIT: YOUR RELATIONSHIP NUMBER

Add your birth path number to your dating partner's birth path number to arrive at your relationship number. (See chapter 12 for more information.) When you examine the challenges and gifts of the relationship number you share with this partner, are you excited about it? Do you feel energized? Or does it deplete you? If you feel excited and energized by looking at the relationship number, that's a good sign. Take another step forward with this partner.

After rating your mate on all of the above qualities, score him one point for success on each of the above five indicators. You get an extra point if the extra-credit exercise was a "yes." A score of five or six means this relationship will be a lasting and positive love in your life—helping you both live up to your great potentials with joy and happiness.

PART

2

SEEING WHAT YOU SIGNED UP FOR

7

REMEMBERING WHO YOU ARE

You did not begin your journey as a physical body. You started as an energy being—a pulsing wave of light—part of the divine fabric of the quantum field that connects all of us.

You CHOSE to take a human lifetime experience as part of your soul's great journey toward divine consciousness. You made a promise to yourself and your posse of loved ones that you would not forget this when you got here.

You promised that you would incarnate into the physical world remembering that this world was your experiment, your playground, a school for learning to manifest divine consciousness. You wanted to help create a consciousness shift here on planet Earth.

Your posse of soul mates agreed they would help. They promised that when you stood powerfully on your path, they would stand beside you.

Imagine this . . .

SIGNING YOUR CONTRACT

I'm sitting in a white, dome-shaped room at a large table. The sound of water falling in the background is soothing. But I'm feeling anxious anyway and am unable to sit still.

The man in front of me carefully studies charts spread out across the table, amused by my impatience. Slowly he looks up and smiles. "You can do this," he says softly. "It's a big path, a strong mission. You're ready."

"What if I get lost? I'm not sure I'm ready."

"You will get lost. But you'll have help from soul mates whom you'll recognize upon meeting." He looks back up at me and smiles. "You know who they are, don't you?"

"Yes, my posse. Same as always." I smile, remembering our great love for one another and our last incarnation together.

"This time, let me caution you: many of those agreements will be designed to spur your growth until you embrace your path and get down to work. Until then, the pain of those relationships will keep you moving. You'll long for a resting place. But it won't appear until you create it with your sacred work."

"What is my true work?" I ask, starting to feel queasy about this journey.

"Using your spiritual wisdom to help others—sharing the gifts you bring in with you to help raise consciousness."

"You think I can do that down there? And get paid for doing it? You DO remember they're still a primitive and economically based world . . ."

"You're up for the job, my dear," he says, staring directly at me with disarming blue eyes.

"Will I be homesick?" I ask.

"And sometimes afraid," he answers. "But these feelings will force you to search for truth and see beyond the illusions. You'll experience pain so you can help others in pain."

"Will one of my soul mates stand beside me to help do the work?"

"Later on, after you've found your strength and courage." He pauses and looks directly at me. "Please remember that you'll never be like others. Many get lost there thinking they should act the same as the others. Each one has his own mission, the sacred work brought to Earth to help shift consciousness. Just remember who you are and focus on your mission."

"Why is there so much confusion in that realm?"

"The dense energy causes us to forget. But that's changing . . ."

"Will I ever have what's considered a normal family life while I'm there?"

He looks back down at the charts and papers spread out before him. He points to a section where several lines intersect. "Oh yes, very sweet . . . but later on."

"How will I remember what I'm supposed to do?"

"Your heart will be broken every time you hide behind a partner. That heartbreak will be your fuel; it will push you forward."

"What about money and comfort?"

"Not really until later. Too much of that in the beginning can slow you down."

"Right . . . no money and comfort until I'm doing the work."

"Right," he says, smiling.

"What clues will I get to help me find my way?"

"Your powerful intuition. You'll see what's coming before it arrives. You'll feel everything around you—good and bad. You'll dream of your partners before they show up. You'll recognize every soul mate the moment you meet. You'll dream about your great work constantly and be restless until you accomplish your mission."

"If I follow my intuition I'll succeed?"

"That's the plan. You'll have to embrace those powerful emotions—loss, anger, fear, joy, and love. Those feelings will help you find your way. Don't worry. We'll be in touch," he says, standing up and moving away from me.

"You'll help when I need you?" I ask, getting up to follow him.

"Through your feelings, dreams, and intuition. I'll see you again so quickly. The visit seems long when you're in it. But it's only the blink of an eye in your soul's journey." He turns and walks out of the room without looking back.

I have more questions and try to follow, but I'm quickly escorted into a large chamber with a platform in the center and told to lie down.

Soothing words and music fill the small space and help me relax. I begin to feel deliciously sleepy. Golden light illuminates from every direction. "It's wonderful," I whisper, lifting my hand up into the light to see the iridescence.

I awaken in a physical body struggling to breathe.

If your life today is not lining up with your soul's mission, perhaps you need a little help remembering who you are and why you're here. Perhaps your pain has overwhelmed you and stopped you from moving forward.

TWO STORIES

These two stories will inspire you to use heartbreak to fuel your great work.

ANGELA'S STORY

Angela was a twenty-four-year-old, Gemini 3 path in a 9 personal year (see chapter 9 to find your path and personal year) when she came to see me as a client. Her career in human resources and as a project manager was unfulfilling and coming apart at the seams. Every morning she spent her hour-long commute dreading the day ahead.

"I hated my job to the point where I was crying in the mirror while getting ready for work and again during my commute. My bachelor's in psychology and my creative dance and art background had all taken a back burner so I could work an acceptable corporate career with benefits."

At the same time, her long-term boyfriend was losing interest in the relationship. He told her he wasn't ready to commit and wanted to see other people. She was desperate to make the relationship work, even though it hadn't made her happy for years. "It wasn't lifting me up, making me giddy, or moving in the right direction. I wasn't sure what I was afraid of, or why I was so bent on making it work when clearly it was not."

To keep the relationship going, she ignored her intuition and shut down her emotions. "I was not honoring myself or my true feelings; instead I was living in fear—desperate for acceptance and love from my boyfriend and at my job.

"I didn't want to get to the root of the issue; I just wanted to feel better," she remembers. But as her 9 personal year unfolded, her boyfriend walked out the door, leaving her to feel the pain of overwhelming heartbreak. It was at this point that she found me and read my book I See Your Dream Job.

During our session, we discussed the need to reconnect with her intuition, stop listening to her overactive brilliant mind, and open her heart. Deepening her spiritual perspective and finding work that inspired her creativity was essential to her Gemini 3 path. I suggested movement like yoga and dance to help her reconnect with her higher self, remember her mission, and quiet her mind.

"I began to look at my life from a different perspective then," she remembers. "It was as if a door opened for me to step through and I had a choice to stay where I was or jump blindly off the cliff, not knowing if something would be there to catch my fall. I learned that the idea of not knowing scared me more than anything, but it had to be better than the place I was in. As I learned to surrender to the energy of my 9 personal year, things began to fall into place. I started listening to my higher self and learned to use my intuition as a compass to guide me."

While still at the job she was unhappy with, Angela began teaching a fitness class at a friend's studio on weekends. "It incorporated all my passions for healing the mind, body, and spirit. This was the reason I had gotten a psychology degree. I was beginning to heal myself by helping others, even though it was only on weekends."

Around this time, her intuition nudged her to quit her job before she was sure how she would make a new income. "I gave my notice with no job and no idea how I was going to make it work," she says.

Angela expanded the number of fitness classes she was teaching and began to bring in more income. After a few months, she felt confident to launch her big dream.

"I decided to open a fitness studio dedicated to the mind, body, and spirit. I wanted a place where people could express themselves and be who they are while exploring new ideas about healing and spirituality."

With her mother's support and money made from teaching at her friend's studio, Angela opened her own holistic fitness center and created a Web site and blog. "I grew more and more passionate about writing, and my blog attracted many readers asking for my counsel. Before I knew it, my classes were filling up. I couldn't believe the flow occurred so quickly."

Today Angela's studio offers her signature fitness and meditation classes, empowerment workshops, and career intuitive counseling. She's successfully and happily making her living from her passion to inspire health and spirituality.

"After I began focusing on my true work, I met my soul mate when I least expected it! And for one of the first times in my life, I could totally and completely be myself without any reservations. I could look in the mirror and honestly tell myself: 'I love you and who you are and what you've learned.' "

Angela met her new love (a Virgo 5 path) while helping her mother buy a car at a dealership. He was the finance director at the dealership. "When I first met him, he was actually the complete opposite of everything I ever looked for in a guy," Angela says.

Angela writes, "He was dressed perfectly; his suit was tailored to show off his tall and slender physique. He was of a different ethnicity, with very dark skin and dark eyes. (He's from Pakistan.) He was incredibly respectful and polite to my mother and me. We felt an immediate closeness, but I was honestly intimidated by his perfectly polished good looks and his perfect jawline. He looked like he should have been modeling for Calvin Klein. Because of my poor self-worth in the past, I had never been drawn to attractive, polished men. But this time, I felt different inside because of the work I was doing and I was more open. My intuition was telling me that he was right. My mother literally encouraged the two of us to date. By our second date, I knew he was the person I was going to be with. I just knew. I felt incredibly comfortable with him, as if I had known him forever. And, I felt incredibly compelled to be 100 percent honest with him 100 percent of the time—which was new for me. I feel like an open book with him; we read each other."

Two years later, Angela is still deeply in love. She believes she couldn't have attracted this fulfilling relationship while in her previous career. "I wasn't being myself in the world so how could I be myself for my partner? I didn't love me, so how could someone else love me?" she says.

"Now I'm doing my true work and living in gratitude, and we're more in love every day," she reports. "I feel a sense of inner peace for the first time in a long time. I've gained respect for myself."

Angela recently wrote to me, "Here's what I've come to believe: doing our true work will lead us to true love. We each have a separate mission, but also a mission together. There are reasons we come back to this physical realm—to learn, teach each other, and share experiences. This is the human experience. When we honor our life path and what we've come here to do we are closer to being 'whole.' I disagree with the famous line from the movie Jerry Maguire, where the character played by

Tom Cruise says, 'You complete me.' We are not one half and one half that comes together to make a whole. You must be whole and complete in yourself to be with your true soul mate. When two complete beings come together, it's the best love anyone could possibly imagine.'"

ANDREA'S STORY

Andrea was a forty-five-year-old, Capricorn 3-path soul with four beautiful teenaged children when her marriage of twenty-four years ended because of her husband's alcoholism. "We lived in a beautiful home, had nice things, and I was well provided for. Yet I was heavily medicated on antidepressants so that I could get up every morning and pretend that life was OK."

Her daily pain and unhappiness inspired her to begin a journey of spiritual awakening that included sessions with me as well as classes in Andean shamanism, a practice Andrea found empowering and heart-opening. This work taught her to love her husband deeply for the person he was and to embrace her own path—whether she stayed with him or not.

When she could finally embrace her husband as a soul on a journey with his own challenges and potential, she was able to release him lovingly and walk away from the security of the marriage.

"I am truly grateful to my former spouse for loving me so much that he spurred a life-changing awakening moment that forced me to dive deep into my soul. The end of our relationship was merely the beginning of everything for me."

When her marriage ended, Andrea was left to examine the life she had created. Raising four kids had kept her busy. Career had been an afterthought—something she had intended to get to when the kids were older. When the divorce was final, she found herself with four kids to feed and very little idea of how to make a living.

"My marriage was over and so was my comfortable lifestyle. I was a single mom with mouths to feed, and I hadn't really worked in twenty years. My spiritual practice helped me turn the helm over to divine guidance with faith that I'd find my way."

Although sometimes the road was bumpy, Andrea trusted her intuition and followed the steps that felt right to her. "As I practiced my spiritual path and dove deeply into it, I came to realize that when I was involved in inner-growth work I felt more like me and more at peace than in any work I'd ever done. I knew then that if I followed this path, I would discover who I was and create the work that was right for me."

Sometimes Andrea worried that this unconventional path of shamanic, intuitive, and spiritual studies she was following wouldn't lead her to a sustainable career. But she held steady to finding what resonated with her. "I was able to reawaken my authentic self, step into my true life path and career, face my darkest fears, remove lots of unresolved pain from my past, and open my heart."

Today Andrea is self-employed as a successful life coach and intuitive energetic healer. She writes books and teaches workshops. "This is what I came here in this lifetime to do. I know this deep within the core of my being. I came to be of service and help others through their transitions, to help people find joy in their lives just as I did. I'm grateful to my former spouse, who on a soul level loved me so much that he gave me the opportunity to find my true self.

"My story doesn't end there," reports Andrea. "One magical Halloween night, I followed my intuitive guidance to attend an event that I wouldn't have normally gone to. That evening my true soul mate (an evolved 9 path), who supports me in every way, serendipitously appeared in my life. I went to the party reluctantly because the dating scene hadn't been working out for me. I was more focused on becoming a career coach and was looking for a client to offer a free practice session to. At the party I met a musician named Peter who said he was looking for a career change. I don't believe in coincidences, so I gave him my card and offered to do a session with him. Later that week when we sat down to do the session, he looked into my eyes and it felt like he was *looking into the depth of my soul. We've been together ever since. With Peter I've learned that my idea of love was so completely different from what love really is. I had no idea how much of myself I tried to hide from the world. This incredible man saw me and loved what he saw exactly as he saw it."*

Andrea says this relationship nurtures her higher self and aids her in doing her great healing work in the world. *"Our love is so much deeper and more fulfilling than anything I've known before. It was definitely worth the journey. I'm so deeply grateful for the broken heart that launched me on this path. Our greatest teachers are those who bring us the deepest opportunities for expansion."*

8

DECIPHERING YOUR SOUL'S INTENTION

You CAME SCREAMING INTO this lifetime with divine energy pulsing through you and a vision of what you were here to accomplish; you KNEW you were a gifted genius who could change the world.

Since that first struggle for breath, you've experienced many challenges, and sometimes they've astounded you. Yet deep inside you've quietly held on to your dream of a meaningful, happy life filled with love and success.

This impossible dream still lives in you for a reason. It's your road map—the plan you brought with you. It's time to brush it off and remember why you're here.

Your life HAS been all on purpose—every moment of it. You programmed each event before you arrived. Your challenges and gifts are penciled in to the fabric of your soul.

But you also brought a powerful tool—your energy. Whenever you use your potent life-force energy to move beyond your pain (rather than getting stuck or giving up), you ALWAYS find your way.

Your moments of deepest pain are designed to help you get where you want to go to live up to your great potential. You chose them perfectly.

This lifetime is uniquely your story; no one else has brought in your exact blend of gifts, dreams, and challenges. It's a personalized plan—designed by you and for you.

Your pain, no matter how potent, is your greatest ally. Its purpose is to fuel you in the right direction—if you let it. Consider the possibility that you've also chosen every wonderful, broken, or painful relationship to open your heart and fuel your great mission. This pattern has certainly been true in my life. Every moment of loss and heartbreak has pushed me to look beyond the surface and embrace my true gifts.

Take a moment and remember the greatest pain you've experienced in this lifetime. Has it been the loss of a loved one? Were you fired or laid off from a career you loved? Has illness or injury sidetracked your life?

Examine your pain story from every angle. Look beyond the illusion of grief, guilt, anger, and blame. What role did you play in this event? What agreement were you fulfilling? What if no one was at fault? What if all the players in your drama were simply performing exactly as you instructed them to—before this lifetime began?

Imagine that your divine guides and departed loved ones are all watching you stomp your foot in anger or sleep your life away. Who are you disappointing really?

Have you gotten lost in your own made-up story? Do you often tell people you were abandoned, injured, rejected, betrayed, abused, fired, disappointed, bankrupted, and generally mistreated by the universe? Perhaps you've confused YOU (a powerful divine-light being) with your story.

Take away the bad guys in your drama. Take away all the people and events you've blamed for your pain. Who is left?

YOU wrote the script, hired the actors, and choreographed every move. You can change the ending. You can still be the hero of your life.

When this life is over and you review it from the other side, what will you see? Someone who never got back up and tried again?

Someone who blamed everyone else? Or will you see yourself as a brave spirit who passionately loved and forgave—and who worked hard to bring your gifts to the world?

The choices you make today determine if this lifetime fulfills your great mission so you can graduate with honors, or if you have to re-enroll and take the course again. Only you can make the choice to graduate.

Let's put a new twist on your story: You weren't abandoned by anyone, ever. You only abandoned your own magnificence. You weren't betrayed by anyone else; you betrayed your own greatness. You weren't abused by anyone. You abused your highest self by not listening to your inner guidance and believing in your powerful gifts.

PAIN AS FUEL FOR A BETTER LIFE

The moment you begin to feel gratitude for your pain (because you realize it's a divine gift to help you find your way), the pain becomes your fuel.

Remember there are no accidents. You chose the players and challenges in your life before you were born. You lined up your lovers, family, friends, teachers, losses, failures, and challenges, so that your greatest potential would be revealed.

The ONLY answer to the question, Why? is "because you chose it for your highest good."

If you've called in lots of challenges, it means you have a strong spirit, and you're here to do great work. The more pain you've experienced, the more powerful you are, and the greater the work you're here to do.

Feel the pain as long as you want to. Just don't get stuck in it. You'll know when your spirit is fed up with the pity party and wants to move on. Don't linger a minute longer in "pitiful."

When a loved one has died, we sometimes feel like we're betraying them if we move on and stop grieving. Yet your loved one is watching from the other realms and desperately wants you to be happy again. Releasing your grief is the greatest gift you can give to someone who has passed on.

If you could have a conversation with your deceased loved one (as I've often had with my departed husband, Paul), he would tell you that your grief hurts him, too. Your painful attachment prevents him from moving on to the great adventure awaiting him in the higher realms.

When Paul died in 1980, Chief Fools Crow (a Native American healer and spiritual guide we visited while Paul was sick) hiked to the nearest phone booth from his cabin in the woods of North Dakota. He lived far from phones and it was long before the days of the Internet, so no one had told him of Paul's death. Yet he knew the moment it happened. He wanted to get word to me through our liaison in Denver.

As I returned home from the hospital, my phone rang. The caller said, "I have a message for you from Chief Fools Crow. He says Paul has passed on now, and the spirit guides are guiding him to higher realms. If you wallow in your grief, you'll prevent him from moving on to where he needs to go to find peace. Let him go."

His words truly helped me; I didn't want to hurt Paul by holding on to my grief, even though I was terribly sad. I would never hinder Paul's progress after everything he had just gone through. I was only twenty-nine years old and might never have moved past my grief if it hadn't been for that powerful realization that if I loved Paul, I had to let him go.

If the person you're grieving for is still alive, but they've chosen not to be in a relationship with you, you have only one option. Let go! You've fulfilled your karmic agreement with this soul and will reconnect at a future time with a new agreement. But you have to let go now or they won't be able to join you again in the future.

Close your eyes and see the person in front of you. Say, "Until we meet again, I release you with love."

ANOTHER STORY TO INSPIRE YOU

Lynn was a fifty-year-old, stay-at-home mom who had been married for twenty-five years when her husband moved out. "I had been devoted to my family and raising children, but somewhere along the way I lost myself," she remembers.

The ensuing divorce, bankruptcy, and selling of her home felt devastating. "I went from a five-bedroom home in a gated community to living in a one-bedroom apartment where I was afraid to walk out the door."

In college, Lynn had studied sociology and child development, but after her divorce, those careers didn't fit. She had such a difficult time getting a job after being out of the workforce for so long that it made her question everything about who she was and what she was supposed to be doing.

Out of desperation, she strung together several part-time jobs to get back on her feet. She knew it wasn't her great work, but she was happy to begin paying bills and living on her terms. Eventually she was able to move into a townhome where she felt safe and comfortable.

The heartbreak she felt every day led her to discover a deep spirituality that she believes gave her strength and guidance. As part of this discovery process, she did a session with me and learned about her powerful master soul path of Cancer 22/4 (see chapter 9 to find your path).

"Now I understand my need for inspiration and purpose in my work, and why my marriage ended. I had forgotten my soul's intention," she says. This realization led her to become a feng shui practitioner and freelance writer.

"My experience has been that when you're in alignment with who you are based on integrity, you're provided with the right opportunities," she says. "I was not on my right path during my twenty-five-year marriage so it ended in divorce."

She recently began a new relationship with a 7-path soul that she says is much more in harmony with who she is and what she's here to do. "I've learned that when you're living your authentic life you attract someone out of strength and honor, rather than out of loneliness or desperation."

Lynn now believes she had a soul agreement with her former husband that was necessary for her evolution. "He was in my life to teach me valuable lessons. I had to learn them or experience that same kind of destructive relationship again.

"The key for me is to be who you're meant to be in the highest form possible. Then you attract the complementary mate. This has had amazing and almost instantaneous results in my life."

MY "BREAK YOUR HEART WIDE OPEN" MEDITATION

If today you find yourself weighed down with heartbreak and grief, this daily meditation will help you move forward. I've used it many times in my life, and it has helped my clients.

1. Start each morning with a ten-minute meditation. During this meditation, quiet your mind with mantra or prayer repetition. I use the mantra *Om Namah Shivaya,* a Sanskrit phrase meaning, "I bow to the highest self." You can also use the Lord's Prayer.
2. At the end of the meditation, when your mind has settled down, ask to feel fully the pain in your heart.
3. Focus your attention on the heart chakra, take several

deep breaths, and allow yourself to experience deeply any pain in your heart. Cry it out if you need to.

4. Picture the pain leaving your heart chakra and moving out of you, up to the divine source. Give it away to God. See divine beings taking your pain away and transforming it into love.

5. Offer to relieve the suffering of humanity. Picture a sick child in an impoverished country. Tell her you'll take her pain so she doesn't have to feel it anymore. Feel her pain and release it to the divine beings. Let them turn it into love.

6. Repeat this meditation again at the end of the day before going to sleep. By starting and ending each day with this process, your grief will dissolve very quickly and you'll have energy to move forward with your life.

9

THE PATH YOU CHOSE

WHEN I STAND IN your presence, I'm taken with your beauty and genius! I feel your unlimited essence and the great intention you brought with you before fear weighed you down.

I'm certain that you came here on purpose to be the hero of your life. I'm certain that you outlined a plan for this journey—a road map with specific destinations highlighted for your visit.

Oh, did you say you were overweight? Did you mention your skin was a different color? I can't remember. It's so hard to focus on the physical form, the temporary costume. It's so irrelevant when your vivid shining grace, your radiant essence, is blinding me. I forget if you said you were an engineer, a doctor, or a murderer. It's all the same to me. My only concern is that you remember you came here on purpose as an angel on a divine mission.

When your heart shatters, leaving remnants of you in pieces—a coat hanging from a tree branch, your favorite sweater wrapped around a pole, a strand of your golden hair spread across the sky— your small mind will open and you'll see a different point of view. The paradox of human life will reveal itself. You'll weep from its beauty. You'll cry to try again. You'll beg the angels to let you stay and help your sister, your daughter, your friend to see everything this new way. You'll forgive your enemy and your lover. The trick is doing this here and now.

I want to help you remember who you are now. When you tell me your date of birth, an intuitive gateway opens, and through that gateway I feel your soul's intention and your pain. I see your gifts. I'm shown a vision of your sacred work and how you intend to help the world. I see you clearly as a divine being here on purpose.

When you speak, I'm always surprised that you don't see this. When you cry, I know it's because your soul is remembering something long forgotten. I watch you struggle to reconcile the vast gap between a fearless divine you and the you that you are today. When you get angry, I know it's because you've worked so hard and gotten nowhere. But, I remind you, it wasn't your true work. It wasn't who you came here to be.

Why don't you see your own divine essence or remember the gifts you brought with you to save the world? You believed it once. Then you let it go, allowed it to slip away beyond your reach, buried under your pain.

Why do you believe the stories that belittle your beauty and diminish your power? Why have you wasted time longing for impossible love when the world so desperately needs your great work? Why are you angry when divine order is always working in your favor? Why do you put so much energy into being ordinary when clearly you're an angel with wings of genius?

As you hurry to the job that belittles you or the relationship that stifles you, I want to grab your arm and say, "Don't be afraid. Your gifts can save you! Remember why you came here."

I wish I could open my soul and wrap you in my vision of your divine essence. But you wouldn't believe me. I've found it's easier to teach you a system that explains logically why you're here and what you came to do. This technique is a number system that will keep your monkey mind engaged in the process of understanding your mission. You can analyze it with your left brain! It's the method the Greek mystic and philosopher Pythagoras developed millenniums ago. Run it through your logic filters because it involves numbers—a code favored by your logical mind.

Pythagoras, the father of our modern number system, first discovered this hidden code in 580 B.C.E., when he created the number system we learned in math class—although our teachers never told us the whole story.

Pythagoras believed that numbers carry an energy or feeling, that they're not just a symbol for quantity. He taught his followers that when you add all the single digits in your date of birth you find your destiny number, which reveals what you've come to accomplish. This destiny number provides a picture of the greatness you came to achieve, along with the potential pitfalls of your path. It reveals the nature of your true work and your many soul-mate agreements.

Once you understand your soul's intention for this lifetime, it explains everything. You realize why you've always carried a big dream in your heart, loved certain people, and hungered for certain opportunities. You also recognize how fear and self-doubt have pulled you off your path and made you question your mission.

Remembering your destined path puts you in the positive, juicy flow of your life. It brings you to love and success. It's the map you've been looking for. And it's all hidden in your birth date.

You may be wondering how your date of birth could be so destined? Perhaps your doctor scheduled your mom's cesarean delivery in his calendar based on his busy practice. Or perhaps you were born three months early. How, you ask, can this be destiny?

Here's the answer: you came here on purpose on YOUR schedule!

Your soul chose the exact moment of entry just as it will choose the exact moment of exit (even though you're not consciously aware of this). When the doctor looked at his crowded datebook and scribbled in the date of your cesarean birth, you were holding the pencil.

Let's explore the powerful truths your date of birth reveals . . .

PYTHAGORAS'S NUMBER SYSTEM

We can reduce all numbers to the digits 1 through 9, except for three cosmic vibrations symbolized by the master numbers 11, 22, and 33.

All other numbers are reduced to the basic digits 1 through 9 by adding the digits of the entire number together.

For example, the number 43 equals 7 (4+3=7).

The number 10 equals 1 (1+0=1).

EXAMPLE OF BIRTH PATH CALCULATION

Birth date: October 16, 1980
Month=October equals 10, equals 1 (1+0=1)
Date=16 equals 7 (1+6=7)
Year=1980 equals 9
9=(1+9+8+0=18) (1+8=9)
Total of month (1) plus date (7) plus year (9) equals 17, which
   equals 8 (8=1+7)
Birth path=8 (1+7+9=17=8)

THE MASTER SOUL NUMBERS

The master numbers of 11, 22, and 33 represent sacred birth paths designed to help humanity evolve. Those numbers are not reduced to a single digit in the final birth path calculations. (But they are reduced to single digits when calculating your final sum. For example, the month of November digits down to a 2 to determine your birth path number.)

EXAMPLE OF A MASTER SOUL BIRTH PATH CALCULATION

Birth date: September 15, 1951
Month=September equals 9
Date=15 equals 6 (1+5=6)
Year = 1951 equals 7
7=(1+9+5+1=16) (1+6)
Total of month (9) plus date (6) plus year (7) equals 22
Total=22 master path soul (9+6+7=22)

The above example is also referred to as a 22/4 path since the 22 is always connected to the 4 path. Similarly, the 11 path is referred to as 11/2 path, and the 33 path is referred to as a 33/6 path.

THREE WAYS OF ADDING BIRTH DATES

It's important to add each birth date three different ways to check your addition and to look for hidden master path numbers.

This is especially important if you've arrived at a 2, 4, or 6 birth path calculation. These birth paths often contain a hidden 11, 22, or 33 path if added two other ways. If the master soul number is "hidden" in this way, it means this person will choose when he or she is ready to step up to do great work—usually later in life.

EXAMPLES

These are the three ways you would add the birth date May 1, 1960, to discover that two out of three ways reveal a 22/4 path while the third way reveals a 13/4.

BIRTH DATE: MAY 1, 1960 = 22/4 PATH

FIRST (TRADITIONAL) METHOD	SECOND METHOD	THIRD METHOD
May = 5	5	5+1+1+9+6+0=22/4
1 = 1	1	
1960 = +7	+1960	
Total = 13 = 4 (3+1=4)	1966 = 22/4	
	(1+9+6+6=22)	

Here is another example of the three methods; this one uses the birth date September 15, 1951.

BIRTH DATE: SEPTEMBER 15, 1951 = 22/4 PATH

FIRST (TRADITIONAL) METHOD	SECOND METHOD	THIRD METHOD
September=9	1951	9+1+5+1+9+5+1=31=4
15 =6	15	(3+1=4)
1951 =+7	+9	
Total =22 (9+6+7=22)	1975=22	
	(1+9+7+5=22)	

Another example of the third method using President Barack Obama's birth date of August 4, 1961:

8+4+1+9+6+1=29=2+9=11

His birth path is a hidden 11/2 master soul path, meaning that 11/2 is the final calculation only when added with the third method. The other two methods both result in a final calculation of 20/2. Because it's a "hidden" master soul number it means he chose when he was ready to step up to do his great work. Until then, he could fit easily into conventional careers without revealing his true spiritual essence.

CALCULATE YOUR BIRTH PATH

Use your date of birth to calculate your birth path according to all three of the methods displayed above:

First method result: _____

Second method result: _____

Third method result: _____

All three methods should arrive at the same final number— even if you discover you're on a master soul path of 11, 22, or 33. Those master-soul-path calculations result in the consistent final combinations of 11/2, 22/4, or 33/6—at least one of the ways you add the birth date. The other two ways may result in various other two-digit numbers that when added together total 2, 4, or 6. (Examples are 20/2, 13/4, or 15/6.)

Your birth month: _____03 = 3_____

Your birth date: _____07 = 7_____

Your birth year: ____1956 = 21 = 3_____

Total: ____13_____

Reduced to a single digit: __4_____

Your birth path number: _____

Note: zero is more than a placeholder in numerology. It's called a potentiator—meaning the zero makes the number in front of it (or behind it) stronger. If your birth path calculation arrives at the number 2020, each zero strengthens the number two in front of it—making this number digit down to a 22/4 master path. The same is true for 1010 or 3030, which become 11/2 and 33/6.

POSITIVE AND NEGATIVE
MEANINGS OF NUMBERS

In Pythagoras's system, every number from 1 through 9 has a positive and negative vibration (which shows its great potential and challenges):

1—Leadership, vision, independence OR loneliness, self-doubt, arrogance

2—Intuition, understanding, detail OR dependency, paranoia, obsession with meaningless details

3—Self-expressive, creative, uplifting OR coldhearted, over-intellectual, irresponsible

4—Self-discipline, strength, determination, practicality OR too practical, lost in drudgery and routine

5—Change, sensuality, freedom, passion OR overindulgence, addictions, impulsive, uncentered

6—Social consciousness, healer, teacher OR slave to others' needs, supercritical of loved ones

7—Intellectual, spiritual focus, wise, dignified, refined OR isolated, hypersensitive, skeptical

8—Power, wealth, accomplishment, generosity OR abusive, manipulative, controlling, hiding from power

9—Humanitarian, accomplished, artistic OR bitter, blameful, focused on past

MASTER SOUL NUMBERS

11—Intuitive, artistic, humanitarian, healer OR too sensitive, egocentric

22—Inspired visionary, practical genius OR greedy, abusive, lost in drudgery

33—Visionary artist, clairvoyant, master healer OR hypersensitive, lost in addictions, disconnected from others

Let's explore exactly what your number means about your mission here on planet Earth.

BIRTH PATH NUMBER 1

What a powerful journey you chose for this lifetime—to stand alone, apart from the crowd as the truth teller, visionary, and leader the world needs. You've had many lifetimes to develop other parts of yourself, but in this one you intended to follow your own voice, truth, and intuition and do it your way—no matter what! Please don't waste time trying to blend in, get lost in the crowd, or hide behind anyone else.

If your life is unhappy and unsuccessful today, it means you need to speak your truth, follow your intuition, and go your independent way—even if that means walking away from security. You'll only find true financial security when you are doing your great work, even if it's unconventional.

It's not an easy journey, but you knew that coming in. So you brought a vast array of gifts to use as your tools for getting it done. These include boundless strength, courage, natural leadership, charisma, honesty, stage presence, brilliance, and independence.

Your challenge, of course, is the opposite of your mission. That enormous pool of self-doubt you dip into daily is also your fuel. Its purpose is to motivate you. You've spent too many nights in the depths of pain—wondering if you're worthy of taking another breath. Let me assure you: we all wait for your vision. We need you to take your place at the head of the line. Don't disappoint us. No one else can do your job and lead us to a better way of living.

This mission requires you to speak up even when that seems the most terrifying thing you can do. The more you share your wisdom, the more powerful your voice becomes—until it becomes the song of compassion and wisdom that changes our world.

At some point, you may decide it's all too hard and lonely and you need to hide out. It's your choice. Every choice can and will be made until you get it right. You'll sometimes struggle to understand where other people fit in your journey. You'll feel wounded when others don't understand your power. You may choose to strike back and hurt them or distance yourself from their love. This will take time and energy and it will lead you offtrack.

Eventually, you'll take your place at the center of the room as the enlightened teacher, the trailblazer, the shaman who guides us to secret knowledge. You're the one we trust to teach us a better way and to help us move past our own self-doubt so that we can fulfill our missions.

Your deep and overpowering insecurity is exactly what you need to push against to stand up and lead the way. You're here to push us forward beyond our limitations and fear. Don't disappoint us, please. We've been waiting a long time.

IN RELATIONSHIPS

You need to stand up for yourself and not crumble in self-doubt. You also need to ask for the space and freedom to realize and follow your independent path. You need a partner who helps you find your voice, own your power, and believe in your unique self and help you bring your true self to the world fearlessly. You're a visionary, a born leader, and you need a partner who isn't afraid, intimidated, or abusive. Your self-doubt is your downfall, so your partner should unconditionally believe in your greatness. Once you get on your powerful path, be careful not to bulldoze everyone in your way or let fear blind you to the gifts of your loved ones.

The right partner will nurture your independence and strength and not be intimidated by you. You need a confident partner whose journey is similar to yours. Your most loving relationship may be with a 5-path soul who is here to be fearless, adventurous, and live outside the rules. An evolved 8 path strong enough to balance you and not become a victim to your power is also a good partner. A loving 9-path soul has your opposite mission but will admire your spunk and independence.

Others with your path include Martin Luther King Jr., Walt Disney, George Balanchine, Truman Capote, Humphrey Bogart, Larry King, Carl Sagan, George Clooney, Janis Joplin, Danny Devito, Sting, Kate Winslet, Sally Field, Hulk Hogan, Anne Heche, Barbara Walters, Tom Hanks, Nicolas Cage, Scarlett Johansson, and Holly Hunter.

BIRTH PATH NUMBER 2

You've had other lifetimes of going it alone and developing your strength. This time yours is a different lesson. Now you need relationships to help you do your great work in the world. You've brought in powerful gifts of compassionate love and great sensitivity. It's time to open your heart.

Yet opening up to relationships may feel like the scariest thing in the world. You won't enjoy being alone either—partly because it won't allow you to do the healing work you have come to do. Your early journey may be so painful that you choose to focus only on organizing the mundane details of life (those that you can control), and you ignore intimacy because it's messy and unpredictable. You may bury yourself in detail work such as computer programming or being a very organized administrative assistant. But it's not what you came to do—even though you're good at it. It's a way of shutting down your heart and hiding from your mission. You've come here to master intimacy and find a deep connection with the divine so that you can be a healer. Opening your heart to feel others' pain is required.

Until you evolve on this path, your deep sensitivity and intuition may wound you and cause you to turn away from the intimacy you crave. As you embrace spiritual knowledge and open your powerful heart, fear will slip away and you'll recognize your sensitivity as your greatest gift for healing others.

You will manifest all your challenges and gifts through your interactions with others in the workplace and at home. You'll have a posse of friends and coworkers who rely on you for counsel. Someday your powerful sensitivity and intuition will inspire you to become a therapist, teacher, or healer. Your most powerful work will be to embrace others in your divine loving energy. Ultimately, you'll become a tower of compassion and support to those you're responsible for and widely recognized for your compassionate sensitivity.

IN RELATIONSHIPS

You'll comfortably fall in sync with your partner and intuitively offer counsel and healing to him. Your life will have most meaning when your partner craves the same level of intimacy and deep connection as you do. He needs to be able to go the distance with you—to be unafraid of feelings and comfortable with your sensitivity. Relationships should be a priority for him as well or you'll feel abandoned and sad. You won't do well with someone who values independence above all else. You might find fulfillment being a therapist or doctor, knowing every day that you've improved someone's life. A wise old 9-path soul whose humanitarian heart is big enough to love you in the way you need to be loved could be your best part-ner. A 4 path is a great relationship for creating a happy home. An-other good choice would be a 6-path soul who loves intimacy as much as you do. If you find a 2 path you're attracted to, the depth of intimacy you crave will become your everyday routine—but so will hurting each other's sensitive feelings.

Others include: my research team and I searched far and wide to find famous 2-path souls. All of the ones we found were actually hid-den 11 paths, which we discovered when we added their birth dates the three different ways. Since divine order is always in action and there are no accidents, I believe that we've evolved to such a fre-quency here that many advanced souls are incarnating in to help raise consciousness as 11-path master souls. They're doing this great work in many mediums, including the arts and politics. Every 2-path celebrity you'll read about in other numerology books is actu-ally a hidden 11 path. If a sacred number such as 11 shows up at the final birth path number when added any of the three ways, it means that soul came here to live up to that 11 frequency at some point in her life and to do work that heals and inspires the world.

In the following section I've listed some of the famous 2-path souls who are actually hidden 11 paths.

MASTER BIRTH PATH NUMBER 11

You came here hungry for inspiration and restless to change the world. You took this highly sensitive, high-frequency path to heal and inspire us with your artistic gifts and intuitive healing energy. You have a huge connection to the other realms that enables you to channel in love, spirituality, and healing for the world.

Your charisma is potent and you vibrate on such an amped-up frequency that it sets you apart; when you enter a room, your en-ergy demands attention. You instantly intuit every feeling present in that room and you sense what everyone is thinking. This is a good thing, though you may not see it as a gift at first. It will sometimes feel as if you're going through life with no skin—vulnerable, exposed, and overwhelmed by feelings.

Without spiritual focus, you may waste your life feeling paranoid, wounded, or trying to please everyone rather than following your own unique mission. Fitting in and being like everyone else is not an option for you.

Find a daily spiritual practice that works for you and do it consistently. I recommend meditation because it quiets your mind and allows you to deepen your pathway to the divine realms. You'll need to establish that connection every day. It will provide the strength needed to overcome your sensitivity, open your heart, and accomplish your great mission.

Your mission is truly unique; your powerful pipeline to divinity can channel in art, music, and healing gifts. You're capable of the highest forms of artistic creation. As a speaker or writer, you'll tap into inspiring ideas the world needs to transform itself. You belong on the stage sharing your spiritual message and inspiring us to live in more enlightened ways. To say you shine is an understatement. Your presence leaves others breathless and open to embrace your message.

If you correctly use these gifts for their highest good, you can change the consciousness of humanity in your lifetime. You'll attract great praise and criticism as you live up to your brilliant path. Be wary of getting lost in tangents or being overly sensitive, or you won't accomplish everything you came to do. Embrace your abundant intuition and trust it to navigate you successfully on this path—overriding your fear and doubt at every turn.

IN RELATIONSHIPS

You need someone with a high frequency like yours who will not think you odd or inferior because you're different. Your partner will need to embrace your sensitivity and intuition and not belittle or dismiss those gifts. He'll encourage your spirituality and help you heal and inspire the world with it. He'll remind you every day of who you are and will pull you away from the details when you get lost. He'll remind you that you can't make everyone happy and that you need to be true to yourself. A 22- or 33-path soul would be good for this reason, but he has his own great work to do and won't be able to support you as much as you need. Your most harmonious connection will probably be with a 22-path soul, so it may be worth the effort to make it happen. Yet a wise 9-path soul will create a sacred partnership with you and support your higher frequency without hurting your feelings. An intuitive and spiritually based 7 path will share your need for meaning and purpose, but his critical nature may wound you. A creative 3-path partner can ease the stress of your great work and offer playfulness as a healing perspective.

Others include President Barack Obama, Michelle Obama, Jacqueline Kennedy Onassis, John Glenn, Katharine Hepburn, Bill Clinton, John McCain, Paul Simon, Meg Ryan, Jennifer Aniston, Orlando Bloom, Emma Watson, Gene Simmons, Kirstie Alley, Julie Andrews, Robert Duvall, Prince William, Prince Charles, Diana Ross, Al Gore, Madonna, Harry Houdini, John Cusack, Stephen Colbert, Colin Powell, and Gwen Stefani.

BIRTH PATH NUMBER 3

You have a brilliant, agile mind, and you came here to inspire the world with your radiant self-expression. Ideas, words, and creativity are essential on your path. These gifts might challenge you in your career. How do you make your living from creative self-expression and brilliant ideas? It's your task to figure that out and make it happen! Many successful dancers, writers, and entrepreneurs are on this path. So don't give up and settle for mundane work that anyone can do.

If you're lost or lonely, it's because you believed what you were told about having to find a secure job with benefits rather than following your unique gifts. Or you've decided it's impossible to make a living from your true talents and you're depending on others to support you.

Your soul's mission involves creativity, artistic expression, and leading others (as a teacher, writer, or entrepreneur) to find their own self-expression. This requires inner work as you quiet your brilliant mind, open your heart, and learn to feel compassion for others. In other words, you need to get out of your head.

Words are essential to the work you came to do. Through exploration of the written word, you'll find your ultimate gift as a speaker and enlightened writer. Your books, inventions, and other works of creativity will someday be held in reverence as examples of great genius and inspiration. Your challenge will be feeling what you feel. Your cerebral viewpoint disconnects you from the world and from your higher self. Physical movement is essential for you; it quiets your overactive mind and reestablishes that connection to your higher self. Try yoga, tai chi, qigong, and other types of healing movement to open your heart energy.

Your gift for movement, music, and visual design makes you an awesome athlete, dancer, designer, musician, or choreographer—as long as you remember to bring your feelings into the work.

Be wary of becoming a financial burden to loved ones, expecting them to provide for you simply because you're brilliant and creative. You're more than capable of making a huge income from your brilliance.

The world needs your voice. You intended to share your powerful gifts through your work—not keep them to yourself. Speaking and teaching are perfect opportunities for moving toward your true work.

You can move energy in a room, on the stage, through your body as a dancer, or through your music and writing. The purpose of these gifts is to heal others in pain. As you mature into this lifetime and learn to cherish your feelings as much as ideas, all your creative endeavors will have a healing intent.

You need a deep spiritual connection to balance out your mind, along with physical movement and exercise to strengthen your intuition. Mental exhaustion can lead you to a spiritual awakening someday when you realize that you can't find all the answers through the mind and that truth lies deep inside your higher consciousness—beyond the limitations of thought.

IN RELATIONSHIPS

You need a partner who embraces your creative self-expression, from your brilliant ideas to your gift of creativity. This partner must be willing to support your creative and intellectual endeavors if you don't want to support yourself financially—even though you're quite capable of doing so. Mostly you need someone to move you out of your head and stop you from analyzing every feeling. The perfect partner will open your heart with passionate love and connect you to your intuition through movement and playfulness. This soul mate will elevate you to the stage where you belong to create income and abundance from your ideas. An evolved 8-path soul may be your greatest love; she can provide the funding you need and will honor your creative gifts (which are so very different from her own). Another 3-path soul is a natural fit for creating a family, as long as one of you can make a living. An inspiring 11-path soul will help you embrace your feelings. A 6-path soul can bring you into family and community for heart-centered connections, and a 1-path soul who is happiest when left to her own independent path will give you lots of space to create and think.

Others include Salvador Dalí; Gloria Vanderbilt; Hillary Clinton; Jennifer Lopez; Winona Ryder; Catherine, the Duchess of Cambridge (popularly known as Princess Catherine); and Queen Victoria.

BIRTH PATH NUMBER 4

You signed up for this lifetime to build emotional, physical, and spiritual strength and discipline. You came here to use that enormous strength to push the world to new levels of achievement. You possess more natural courage, honesty, and determination than others. Your best choice is to embrace the challenge of hard work as your opportunity for spiritual and emotional growth that will someday change the world. Try not to get overwhelmed.

A positive attitude will lead to great happiness and success. The courage and strength you build in this lifetime will serve you and the world as you use them to accomplish feats impossible for others. You may need to soften the edges of your determination and allow yourself to be vulnerable to experience love.

If you're lonely today, chances are good that you've gotten lost in the drudgery of your work and feel victimized and powerless. Yet you're one of the most powerful beings on the planet!

Your strength, focus, and willpower can accomplish any challenge, from climbing Mount Everest to running a newsroom or to building homes from scratch. You always get it done, no matter how big the job or short the deadline. You're meant to pursue and succeed at impossible dreams when others can't. Never limit your expectations and always say yes to challenges.

You'll be drawn to others with strength and fortitude, and you'll have little patience for trivia and superficiality. You'll feel happiest when pushing yourself to physical and mental extremes. This exertion makes you feel powerful and alive.

I suggest massive doses of physical exercise and movement to keep you happy and healthy. The worst course of action for you is to do nothing. Inactivity creates huge discordance and self-doubt since it's not what you came to experience this time around. It makes you feel weak—which is not in alignment with your mission.

Practicality, self-discipline, strength, and determination are your gifts, yet if you become too practical, you can lose your way. You will forget you're a spirit on a journey, which will cause you to shut down your feelings and perhaps keep you from experiencing true love.

Whenever you feel victimized and overworked, embrace your spiritual nature. This step will help you see the bigger picture and choose tasks worthy of your great fortitude and dedication.

With your logical mind and great ability to concentrate, you pare things down to their essential nature. In other words, you see and speak the truth without hesitation. This honesty will serve you and get you in trouble. You may be disappointed in others who don't speak the truth and have less integrity than you have. They'll catch you off guard because you assume the same good intentions in others as you carry in this lifetime.

Your trusting nature and enormous sense of responsibility are unique, and you'll realize eventually how rare these gifts are. Be careful whom you trust—especially as a partner. Follow your intuition when choosing work projects and loved ones and you will ensure that you'll be using your terrific determination to accomplish your great work.

IN RELATIONSHIPS

You need someone with great integrity and a strong sense of humor who understands and supports hard work. He'll cherish your strength and determination and believe wholeheartedly in your career. He'll need to be happy to take a second slot to your overwhelming workload. As long as he believes in your work passionately, he'll enjoy the journey with you—but he needs wisdom and insight to support your efforts. Most of all, your partner must be able to pull you out of your drudgery and create laughter, fun, and relaxation in your hard-working life. Don't be seduced by the sensuality of the 5-path soul; your mission of truth and accomplishment is not in harmony with his journey of adventure and addiction. Find a brilliant, intuitive 7 path who will offer the dialogue and deep understanding you need for this journey. You'll be drawn to nest with an 11-path soul whose wisdom can heal you. An evolved 8 path with the ability to make you laugh may be best to stand powerfully at your side and cherish your hard work.

Others include Usher, Nicole Richie, Jennifer Hudson, Jewel, Jake Gyllenhaal, Demi Lovato, Kate Hudson, Christian Slater, Joss Stone, and Hilary Swank.

MASTER BIRTH PATH 22

You'll be driven to do something great with your life from the time you're very young. Your great restlessness will push you to take on huge challenges. You'll be acutely aware of your unique perspective and how it differs from mainstream thought. All of this may make you doubt yourself at first, but it will eventually fuel you to move forward and succeed at something that inspires and changes the world.

If today you find yourself heartbroken, it's because you've tried to fit in and be someone you're not. You've hidden your unusual gifts in order to be loved. Yet hiding out prevents you from being loved!

There is nothing average or "normal" about you. Your frequency is several notches higher, more attuned and intuitive than anyone else around you. Because of this you may be given labels such as ADD or bipolar, but don't be deterred. There is nothing wrong with you!

First, you must find your spiritual practice and use it every day as your fountain of inspiration and power. This will help you navigate a world that seems crazy from your perspective. Sharing your unique viewpoint is your true work!

When you open your heart and share the enormous love you carry for humanity, it wraps the world in peace and forgiveness. When you shut down, your cold power wounds everyone around you.

You won't ever want to settle for a mundane career—and that's on purpose. You don't belong there. When you take that path, it never works out. Your high-frequency presence sabotages all attempts at having a conventional life. That's a good thing!

Your vision of a better world is your gift. Don't dismiss it or waste time criticizing the way things are now. Tap into your enormous pool of inspiration and find a way to use your vision as the foundation for your work. That mission is the one you came to share.

When you aren't feeling inspired by your work, it's time to reinvent. You need partners and friends whose conversations leave you feeling uplifted and inspired to do something bigger.

You'll have the strength of the 4 combined with the inspiration and brilliance of the 22. Use that amazing combination to accomplish your mission—making significant, inspired contributions to the way we think and live our everyday lives.

Your powerful 4-path strength is necessary for this journey, so be sure to nurture your physical health through exercise and healthy food. Alternatives will always attract you—especially alternative medicine, which you'll find very helpful in this lifetime.

Your work is to teach the most enlightened new principles of forward thinking. Always think bigger and seek out leaders who will open their doors to you. Your salvation lies in seeing the big picture, following your inspiration, opening your heart, and not getting lost in details, drudgery, or routine.

Your highest work requires stepping out of the confines of convention—into alternative worlds of knowledge, spirituality, intuition, and healing. You're creating a body of work that will be honored and followed long after you exit this life.

IN RELATIONSHIPS

You need someone who makes you laugh and remember your spirituality even when the workload is overwhelming. Your partner needs a brilliant mind and a deep respect for your work, spirituality, and intuition. She'll share the journey of bringing your great work to the world—not as a bystander but as a cocreator in your ideas, inspiration, and decisions. She'll need to pull you out of the trenches many times to remind you of the bigger picture. She must embrace her own spiritual mission and intuition profoundly enough to provide strong support for you and your work. And she must make you laugh, relax, and enjoy life whenever possible.

A great choice would be a spiritually evolved 7 path who will happily explore unknown worlds with you or a loving, intuitive 11 path who holds you in the highest light for your work. You'll be drawn to 22-path partners, but they'll be too busy with their own work to support you in yours. An enlightened 8 path can open doors for you in the world of success. A wise old 9 path with a powerful heart would give you a sweet resting place.

Others include Henry Ford, Paul McCartney, Linda McCartney, Hugh Hefner, Mike Nichols, Clint Eastwood, M. Night Shyamalan, Brad Pitt, Oprah Winfrey, Arnold Schwarzenegger, Bono, Desmond Tutu, Barbara Bush, Demi Moore, Will.i.am, Nicole Kidman, Elton John, Bill Gates, Donald Trump, Will Smith, Leonardo da Vinci, and Pamela Anderson.

BIRTH PATH NUMBER 5

There's no one on planet Earth more attractive, compelling, and charismatic than you are. You can light up a room. That's on purpose. Your physicality serves you by attracting boundless opportunities for learning, which helps you fulfill your soul's true intention. Early years may include sexual or physical abuse. It's part of your sweet nature and compassionate spirit to accept others no matter who they are. Your sexuality will provide many opportunities for growth as you learn your greatest lessons through the body.

Your powerful sensuality and passion are all designed to open your heart. Your mission is to drink fearlessly from the cup of life—learning everything there is to learn about the physical realm and experiencing it through every cell. Earthly pleasures, from food to music and drugs, will seduce you and you may sometimes get lost in self-indulgence and addictions.

If you're alone today, it may be because early childhood pain and abuse caused you to shut down your wide-open spirit and hungry heart. It's time to wake up. You came to this lifetime to embrace courage and passion and to step out of bounds. You're capable of sharing powerful love and healing through your work, but fear will shut this love right down until your life force is nearly diminished. Then you'll fall far off path.

Everyone will be attracted to you. Abundant opportunities will flow in your direction. These circumstances will teach you to make right choices for your soul's evolution and your highest good. Though you may choose the experiential school of hard knocks to learn these lessons, it's not necessary if you trust your boundless intuition. You sense everything and know things you shouldn't know. Trust that. It's your inner guidance system trying to make the journey easier. Your mind is unreliable, but your gut is always right.

You're definitely not suited for routine or convention. Freedom, expansion, adventure, and fearlessness feed your soul. Change is your most powerful ally. Embrace the energy of adventure and courage since that's what you came to master. Say yes to new experiences even when they scare you. Your acceptance of these challenges will put you on your true path.

You'll find salvation in a rich spiritual perspective that grounds you in health and sanity. Only then will you be able to fulfill your intention of serving others who lose themselves in fear and illusions. However, embracing spirituality will be tough for you at first, since you tend to believe only in what you can see, touch, taste, and hear. You may have to hit bottom from physical indulgences before you look beyond the physical world for meaning and purpose. Your great work will provide love and nurturing for those who've fallen off the edges. Your powerful compassion can heal the world when you let it.

You belong in the alternatives—from alternative health careers to adventurous travel and outdoor lifestyles. Yet you need meaning and purpose to anchor you, or life will become chaotic and might make you sick.

Ultimately, you're here to help those who struggle with addiction, fear, or lack of spiritual focus. You'll provide healing and comfort for those who flounder on the fringes of life and help them find purpose and meaning as you've found yours. You'll be the light of encouragement and truth for the world when you share your powerful and unconventional wisdom.

IN RELATIONSHIPS

You need a partner of great spiritual depth and insight—a highly evolved wise and spiritual soul who does not judge and instead offers wisdom and counsel. He'll need the strength to pull you through your addictions, indulgences, and passions—in particular your propensity to learn all your lessons through the flesh. Not only must he have the spiritual depth to help and counsel you, he also must join you in your sensual passions, cherishing passion and adventure as much as you do. If not, you'll turn elsewhere for sexual expression, since that's a huge part of your evolution in this lifetime. You may benefit most from an independent 1-path soul who gives you all the space you need to fight your battles and learn your lessons. You may find an anchor in that 1-path partner's solid strength and wisdom.

Yet a loving 6- or 33/6-path soul could be your greatest, most lasting love. A wise and spiritually evolved 7-path soul will be fun for a while. You'll be drawn to a 3-path soul's creative spark, but unless he's highly evolved and spiritually strong, there won't be enough depth to keep you interested.

Others include Rudolf Nureyev, Marlon Brando, Lana Turner, Uma Thurman, Isabella Rossellini, Catherine Zeta-Jones, Ron Howard, Angelina Jolie, William Faulkner, and Mark Zuckerberg.

BIRTH PATH NUMBER 6

Your beauty and grace are angelic and give you rock-star charisma that you can use to either heal the world with your enormous heart or slide down a dark path of self-indulgence and self-destruction. It's your choice, and you may need to experience both sides before choosing to heal the world.

Your boundless gifts—especially the creative ones—allow you to pursue the path of the artistic genius or gifted dancer or athlete. You have profound intuition and the ability to sense energy. But without spirituality as your anchor, you may become untethered and unsuccessful.

If you're alone today, it may be because you've lost yourself in your partner's needs and forgot to be YOU. It may also be because you forgot that your heart is for healing others' pain. Only you hold the great love you're seeking. Shine that love and compassion out to everyone you meet and your life will blossom.

Ultimately, your soul's evolution occurs when you open your powerful heart and feel compassion, even for the imperfections of humanity. You'll heal and inspire your family, community, and world—moving from indulgent artist/athlete to enlightened healer/teacher/politician. You may not realize your greatest work until later in life.

True spirituality must be at the core of your life to keep you from crazy obsessions and focusing on others' imperfections. Your global consciousness will inspire you to work for justice and social causes, but you can get lost in the anger and blame of self-righteousness and risk becoming fanatical and destructive if your spiritual core isn't strong.

Home and family are essential to your happiness, and you may marry young. Beware of losing yourself in family needs and forgetting to grow as a person. If you're not healed, you can't help anyone else. You must remember who you are and get your own needs met to be fulfilled and happy.

IN RELATIONSHIPS

You need someone to spark your creativity and match your powerful intellect. But she must also be wise and intuitive to join you on this heartfelt journey. You need a partner who will pull you out of your focus on the world, the community, and the needs of others to remind you to focus on who you are. She'll be able to explore great artistic and philosophical ideas with you, enter into a truly committed partnership and family, and appreciate your healing and artistic gifts without being intimidated by your rock-star beauty.

You may find your truest love in a 5-path soul—if she's evolved and spiritually aware. A 9-path soul with a strong humanitarian focus can help you concentrate on service rather than fanaticism, and she'll provide a loving home for you. A 3-path soul will engage your artistic side but leave your heart hungry for deeper connection. You'll be drawn to 22-path souls, but unless you're already doing your true work and embracing your highest self, they may push you too hard.

Others include John Denver, John Lennon, Meredith Vieira, Britney Spears, Justin Timberlake, Al Franken, Sarah Palin, the Reverend Jesse Jackson, Richard Nixon, and Goldie Hawn.

BIRTH PATH 33

The highly evolved, enlightened, and sensitive path of the 33 is sometimes called the Christ path. You have the highest frequency a soul can carry in this physical realm. This situation can be good and bad. You chose this path to use your love, wisdom, talents, and clairvoyance to transform consciousness through your work. It's a big task, but you're completely capable of success.

You're loaded with personality, beauty, and charisma on purpose. You have the most compassionate heart found on planet Earth and you came here for big spiritual development for yourself and the world. As an artist, you have an unfettered pipeline to inspiration and an unmatched ability to download whatever guidance you desire for your creations.

If relationships haven't worked out, you're probably not picking partners with high enough frequencies to support you as a divine healer and teacher. Or you've forgotten who you are and tried to fit in the conventional world—a strategy that has pulled you far from your sacred mission.

When you finally become a healer or gifted artist, you'll be the clairvoyant, shaman, energy master, and intuitive who creates a new form of spiritual healing for the world. If you focus on this task, you can put an end to all disease of the body and soul.

Your challenge is as great as your gifts. With your unrestrained clairvoyance, intuition, and sensitivity, falling off the edges of the world is a definite possibility. This is why you must ground yourself in the highest spiritual awareness, stay far away from dark arts, and never touch a drop of alcohol or drugs. These vices can make your mission unobtainable and fill you with delusions that waste your time here on Earth.

IN RELATIONSHIPS

You need someone who carries a similar high frequency and who has enough spiritual wisdom to support you fully on your highly sensitive, gifted journey. You don't have much of a tether to this physical realm, and your true partner reminds you every day of the reason you dance in the ethers—to bring spiritual and intuitive guidance to the world. He won't encourage your addictions but rather heal them with words of wisdom and compassion. He'll recognize your charisma and artistic gifts, but he'll also realize those gifts must be used to make a difference in the world or you'll lose your way through psychosis or addiction.

A spiritually evolved 9-path soul can support you emotionally and won't be afraid of your unusual gifts. You'll fall deeply in love with a 5-path soul, but unless he's ready for true spiritual focus, it won't last. If you can find an evolved 5 path who has already learned his lessons from addiction, it will be a perfect fit. An 11- or 22-path partner will understand you in ways no one else can, but he'll be too busy with his own work.

Others include Lindsay Lohan, Charlie Sheen, Meryl Streep, Jude Law, Barry Bonds, Robert De Niro, Tom Waits, George W. Bush, Lenny Kravitz, Ho Chi Minh, Dean Cain, Bruce Willis, Rudolph Giuliani, Katherine Heigl, Roman Polanski, Caroline Kennedy, Steven Tyler, Melissa Etheridge, Christopher Reeve, and Ben Affleck.

BIRTH PATH NUMBER 7

You chose this lifetime to bridge the physical and divine realms, to live in the physical world without losing your spiritual connection. Your greatest work is to meld these two worlds through art, music, and intuition. Your brilliant creativity comes from your unique ability to channel inspiration from the highest realms. This gift can change the world if you allow it to manifest completely through your work.

You're hungry for the truth, and, from the time you were very young, you've been intent on learning why things are the way they are. Your insatiable intellect has pushed you to pursue the highest knowledge. Spirituality (not religion) will someday heal your sensitive soul and lift you out of cynicism. Embracing love rather than sarcasm opens your creativity and fuels your great work.

If you find yourself alone or unloved, it's because you're shut off from your own spiritual connection. You, more than anyone, need your spiritual pipeline opened up and flowing freely. Without it, you can become a negative, bitter, fearful perfectionist, finding flaws in anyone who gets close—terrified of this world and its unpredictable experiences.

Your goal is to learn that true perfection only exists in the highest realms and not here in the physical world. This lesson could take your entire lifetime to master because you're so driven to find perfection in the details. Yet this endless pursuit of meaningless perfection never makes you happy.

Your exceptionally refined energy makes you unsuited for most big business careers. Your pristine mind, which is capable of great learning, will urge you into finance, law, science, or religious studies, where you're encouraged to ask, Why? But even those fields will eventually feel limited and restrictive.

Your hunger for the truth is unrelenting and purposeful. It will drive you to recognize that intuition and spiritual wisdom are your greatest gifts. Once you embrace that knowledge, anything you want to accomplish is possible.

Spending time outdoors in nature will probably be your first step toward embracing your higher self. You don't truly belong in this world and much of the goings-on here will disgust you, but you came on purpose to help raise consciousness. Remember you're a visitor with a divine mission and don't get pulled into the drama.

The spiritual and mystical will always call you, and therein lies your ultimate fulfillment. You'll be happiest when you have plenty of time alone to reconnect to your higher self.

Ultimately, you'll be the wise artist, writer, spiritual guide, and sacred teacher. You'll translate divine knowledge for the rest of us without having to live and work in the fray of human struggle.

IN RELATIONSHIPS

You need a partner who loves analyzing, philosophizing, and discussing who we are, why we're here, and what it's all about—someone to join you in the search for higher meaning. Your partner must deeply embrace spirituality, intuition, and hunger for higher consciousness and pull you away from cynicism and doubt. Although you love beauty and perfection, you're only truly drawn to the depth of someone's soul and how she uses her brilliance to pursue higher knowledge. Your true partner helps you release your focus on details to see the bigger picture. She helps you realize that perfection does not exist in the physical world—only in the unseen worlds. She helps you embrace your true intuitive gifts and use them in your life and work.

Your best choice is an evolved 22-path soul whose mission inspires you to be your best self. An 8-path soul can provide financial security so you can pursue your higher calling and raise a family. You'll be drawn to a wise old 9-path humanitarian, but it may feel empty eventually. A beautiful 5-path soul will attract you, but unless she's highly evolved, you'll soon get bored.

Others include Andy Warhol, Leonard Bernstein, George Harrison, Julia Roberts, Paula Abdul, Johnny Depp, Christian Bale, Al Pacino, and Hugh Grant.

BIRTH PATH NUMBER 8

You're a brave, wise old soul, and you've already developed great spiritual wisdom and genius in other lifetimes. When you chose this incarnation, you embraced the most difficult lesson that humans can take on: how do I own my power in every area of life and use it generously to empower others? Every lesson of this lifetime will be embodied in that simple question.

If you find yourself alone, it's because you fell into the negative use of power and became abusive or manipulative—or you avoided power by playing the victim and hiding out. Either way, this misuse of energy will destroy relationships and steer your life far off course.

Yet every time you take a step to own your greatness, you'll meet with huge success—bigger success than most people will ever know. This is your lifetime to master the game of money (rather than avoiding it), since that's the ultimate power challenge. You're more than capable of doing this even though it terrifies you.

On this journey, you'll experience every pitfall from abuse and manipulation to sabotage and greed—until you get it right. Ultimately, you'll learn from these challenges and become abundantly successful, respected, and generous.

The only way to succeed at this mission is to step up to the plate. Thinking big is your only option. In this lifetime, you're not allowed to hide out for very long in any area of your life. You will be called to stand up for yourself in every relationship starting from childhood.

Since you're here to experience great wealth and power, many opportunities to head in that direction will come your way. Just say yes even when you're afraid. Someday your success will enable you to do your greatest work—funding the causes you care about and helping millions of people who struggle in fear and poverty. Then you'll have come full circle to fulfill your soul's intention for this lifetime. You'll have mastered one of the final and hardest lessons of human incarnations.

IN RELATIONSHIPS

You need a partner who will not upstage you and sees you as the powerful being you came here to be. This partner recognizes your challenge of using power to empower others and helps you learn to do that. He doesn't allow you to play victim, be abusive, or be stingy. He sees your greatness and teaches you to own it. Yet he's as powerful as you are, which means you're not tempted to be abusive or manipulative. This partner needs physical strength and charisma as well as inner strength. He'll stand beside you encouraging your generosity, truth, and spiritual focus.

A good choice could be the powerful and independent 1 path or the physically charismatic 5 path. You'll also be drawn to the hard-working 4 path, whose strength you'll admire and learn from. A 3-path soul will provide spark and energy as well as love and trust. A 7-path soul will help you embrace your highest self and create a harmonious home.

Others include Pablo Picasso, Muhammad Ali, Jane Fonda, Tennessee Williams, Stanley Kubrick, Paul Newman, Lucille Ball, Joan Crawford, Shannon Tweed, Martha Stewart, and Matt Damon.

BIRTH PATH NUMBER 9

This ultimate-realization lifetime will tie up the loose ends of your karma and teach you to live in tune with your highest self so you can pass your soul's final exam. You'll be asked to face heartbreak with compassion, loss with understanding, and disappointment with wisdom. It's time to realize you're always the wise old soul in the room, here to guide others. That task carries responsibility. Take your place on the stage and teach your wisdom to others. You still have a huge humanitarian mission to accomplish, and it's time to do it.

If you're alone today, ask yourself if it's because you let loss and disappointment turn you into a bitter, blameful person and you thus forgot to do your great humanitarian work in the world. If you can truly say that you've released past grudges and disappointments, true love is on its way!

You're worldly, charismatic, and brilliant enough that on the surface you look great. But deep inside is where the true work is needed—to release the blame, arrogance, bitterness, and cynicism you still carry inside from painful past incarnations. To help you fulfill that mission, this lifetime will present many great teachers and opportunities for growth. You'll have many broken relationships to heal. Feeling your pain and releasing it to its highest good will open your heart to true love.

The charisma and skills you've gathered over so many lifetimes may confuse you—causing you to waste time in addictions and pleasures attracted by your personal charisma rather than getting your true work done. Your free spirit, enormous creativity, broad knowledge, wisdom, and compassion will make you the center of attention, but you must use this power for good rather than manipulation.

Forgiveness and gratitude will serve you every day on this journey. Each time you master an inner challenge, your life will unfold in a joyful way as you prepare to exit your cycle of human incarnations. To graduate, you must surrender to your highest self and open your heart.

Inspire others with your compassion for the human condition and your deep understanding of spiritual truths. Your great work is always humanitarian and service-oriented. Mysticism, music, and art intrigue you because of your ability to tap into the divine realms.

Don't look back and count injustices. Practice sacred amnesia to forget anything or anyone who has ever wounded you. Reach for the future and finish this lifetime with grace and wisdom. You always intended to finish it strong.

IN RELATIONSHIPS

You need a partner who sees beyond the illusion of the physical world and has personal access to spirituality and intuition. This partner will dance with you in this great lifetime—rising above challenges with compassion, love, and wisdom. She'll understand your pursuit of consciousness and growth. You'll be drawn to those on high-frequency paths such as 11, 22, and 33. And you'll have many soul mates on those paths.

An evolved 11-path soul may be your greatest love. Yet comfort will come from the playful 3-path soul who helps you analyze the meaning of life. A spiritual 7-path soul will resonate deeply. A 6-path soul will build a loving home for you. But a 1-path soul may attract you most of all. As long as this 1-path soul has moved beyond self-doubt to pursue her great work, you could find a permanent loving partnership with her.

Others include Frank Lloyd Wright, Elvis Presley, Charles Lindbergh, Yoko Ono, Shirley MacLaine, Robert Redford, Whitney Houston, Jimi Hendrix, James Van Praagh, Jimmy Carter, and Harrison Ford.

THE FLAVOR OF YOUR BIRTH PATH

How do the numbers in your birth date interface with astrology? In many ways. However, we're keeping it simple here and only focusing on the sun sign's influence.

Your sun sign reveals the overriding flavor of your life and work. By combining your birth path number and sun sign, you'll get a Gestalt impression of what you came here to do and how you'll do it.

For example, someone on a 7 birth path with an Aries sun sign will fulfill his destiny with a different style than someone on a 7 birth path with a Pisces sun sign. But their souls share the same intention and their great work fulfills the same mission.

Let's learn more about this . . .

SUN SIGNS

Aries (Ram) March 21–April 19
Taurus (Bull) April 20–May 20
Gemini (Twins) May 21–June 21
Cancer (Crab) June 22–July 22
Leo (Lion) July 23–August 22
Virgo (Virgin) August 23–September 22
Libra (Scales) September 23–October 23
Scorpio (Scorpion) October 24–November 21
Sagittarius (Archer) November 22–December 21
Capricorn (Goat) December 22–January 19
Aquarius (Water Bearer) January 20–February 18
Pisces (Fish) February 19–March 20

ENERGY OF THE SUN SIGNS

Aries (Ram) March 21–April 19

If you wrapped your birth path number with Aries, it means you didn't come here to hide out, play it small, or humbly do your work. You came to be powerful and bold like the sun—leading us into the light of understanding and healing. Shining your light on fear and transforming it to love is your only path to true success. Be careful not to overpower your partner with your enormous presence. Shine your light on others to illuminate their beauty as well as your own.

Taurus (Bull) April 20–May 20

If Taurus is the flavor you chose, you're made of pure force and solid willpower. Being practical puts you at ease, but it's also your stumbling block. You grip too tightly to mundane ideas. Practicality can become your most cherished value at the cost of everything else—including love. Be aware that your stubbornness can ruin relationships. Opening up to new ideas and growth is required. You'll take a while to get going on your higher mission; it's essential that you open your heart to the bigger meaning of life to fulfill your potential and to remember who you truly are—a spirit on a journey.

Gemini (Twins) May 21–June 21

Your agile, hungry mind is a great gift, but it's also your Achilles' heel. Your monkey mind will make you doubt your intuition and ignore what your higher self wants and needs. You'll change perspectives frequently and become quite brilliant, cunning, and accomplished. But the coldheartedness that goes along with that great mind will not serve you and it will destroy true love in a heartbeat. Your challenge is to stay true to your partner even when you get a different idea of what you want in your relationship. You must meditate every day to quiet your mind and open your heart. Let your heart and intuition serve as your compass, or you'll lose your way and fall off path.

Cancer (Crab) June 22–July 22

Your heightened sensitivity, powerful emotions, and secretive nature are your gifts and your challenges. You feel everything and process it all through a silent filter, rather than readily sharing it with others. Yet your feelings and intuitions are on purpose. They'll guide you accurately in all your decisions. You're meant to use your big love to help others. Don't hide that brilliant wisdom and retreat into self-doubt and fear. Be aware that your fear destroys relationships. Show your sensitivity to the world, bare your sweet soul, and speak the truth. Coming out of your shell and shining love on others is required for any successful relationship or career.

Leo (Lion) July 23–August 22

You came into this lifetime to help and heal with generosity of spirit and a fiery passion for the truth. Your confident charisma will dominate any environment, from home to the workplace. But it's easy to get lost in empty showmanship. It's a cliché to call you the cowardly lion, but it fits when your roar is shallow and meaningless because you haven't dug deep enough into your essence to find your spiritual core. Without that core, your power is pointless, even destructive—especially in relationships, where your fiery essence can fuel temper rather than passion. But your heart is enormous, and whenever you shower your loved ones with compassion and acceptance, you heal them. That healing energy is required in all your relationships or you'll never get the love you want. Reach deep for the purpose of this great path—lighting the fire of higher knowledge and compassion.

Virgo (Virgin) August 23–September 22
You came here to experience the searing, truth-seeking energy that dominates a Virgo lifetime and ultimately to discover and share great knowledge that the world needs for its evolution. Your relentless analysis and pursuit of perfection is your gift and curse. If you stay stuck in your head, you'll ignore your intuition and dismiss your highest self. The best antidote to your laser-honed, fault-finding mind is daily meditation, which will open your heart and tap in to your intuition. In any career, you'll get to the core of the problem and perceive the essential truth instantly. Your challenge is to refrain from pointing out those flaws and imperfections until you've found compassionate solutions to share. This is especially true in relationships, where you can either destroy or empower by your choice of perspective. Realize that you hold the love and understanding that your partners need to evolve to their highest potential. When you move from judge to enlightened teacher, you'll finally receive the love you need to heal yourself.

Libra (Scales) September 23–October 23
Grace, beauty, truth, and fairness flavor your mission and relationships. It's what you came to learn. Your need to see both sides of everything can paralyze you and shut down your heart. Yet your feel-

ings lead you to the truth and help you make good choices. Trust them. Rather than focusing on injustices, create solutions. Your abundant talents will find a home in the arts—whether you choose acting, dance, writing, or design. Your partner will need to love the arts, philosophical ideas, and deep discussions as much as you do. And she'll need to help you open your heart whenever you're stuck in your head or lost in indecision. Remember that love is not an idea. It's a feeling. And that feeling is something your partner needs from you.

Scorpio (Scorpion) October 24–November 21

No matter what you're here to accomplish, this sun sign will flavor your path with intensity, sexuality, and charisma. Use those gifts to shed light on the unseen world and guide others through traumatic pain (which doesn't intimidate you). You love to dive beneath the surface where others fear to go. And you may prefer sexuality to love—but beware of this weakness. Learn to love with compassion and not just passion. As you evolve, your healing and insightful visions will carry a depth of wisdom that the world needs. Don't get lost in your search for meaning. Instead, use your powerful intuition, compassionate heart, and flawless insight to be the ultimate healer for those in pain. You need a partner who embraces your passion and is not afraid of how deeply it consumes you. He'll help you enjoy life and embrace your spiritual nature as the source for your true work.

Sagittarius (Archer) November 22–December 21

You came to learn the art of social connection, and your friendly charisma puts everyone at ease. You can start up a conversation with anyone—from the president of the United Nations to a computer nerd. But don't let your social personality pull you from your mission and sidetrack you. Your social gifts are on purpose—to help you succeed as a teacher and visionary. Dig deep to open your compassionate heart and find your spiritual truth. Share your powerful insights even at a dinner party. If you spend too much time in the superficial small talk that comes so easily, however, your life will be wasted. Your gregariousness is perfect for teaching the highest truths of our shared human experience. Remember, you're the shaman at the cocktail party, not the gossip girl. Don't be afraid to speak truth. Your charisma and presence are perfectly designed to get people listening to you. In relationships, you'll need to learn when to stop talking and to start feeling. The enormous love and compassion that waits inside of you are the key to successful partnerships. Be quiet and open your heart, and you'll receive all the love you've longed for.

Capricorn (Goat) December 22–January 19

You came here to immerse yourself in the earthy, practical details of day-to-day reality and learn to accomplish great things in this realm. But your one-pointed focus can also hurt you. You'll miss the big picture and may nitpick your relationships to shreds. Your gift of plodding determination needs to be pointed in the right direction, or you'll go in circles accomplishing nothing of true merit. Loosen your grip on mundane details. Learn to feel what's in your heart even though you prefer living in your head. You're smart, charming, and cunning enough to get by in life without ever looking beyond the surface. But this shallowness is your Achilles' heel and will prevent you from accomplishing the larger healing work you came here to do. Loving others in spite of their imperfections is required. Open up to the less practical ideas of spirituality and intuition that, until now, have made you feel uncomfortable. This expanded awareness will help you fulfill your great potential. Embrace true love in spite of its impracticality; it will open your heart—a necessary step for accomplishing your mission.

Aquarius (Water Bearer) January 20–February 18

Your ability to teach and inspire others with new ideas is paramount on this path. Use these great strengths to change the world. Take classes, read great books, surround yourself with thought-provoking people—and then get out of your head and into your gut. Daily meditation and physical exercise will help you embrace your feelings and use spirituality as your compass. This is necessary to open your sexuality for deep connection with a partner. At your worst, you're a walking encyclopedia or a manual on how to live a good life—lecturing anyone who will listen. But your heart is another story. Unresolved anger will begin to consume you unless you embrace your emotions and open your heart. Whether you begin your career as a journalist or healer, you'll end up teaching what you know. It's as natural as breathing for you, and the world needs your inspired instruction. But in relationships, you need to surrender what you know and become vulnerable. Consider yourself the student when it comes to love. Allow your partner to be the teacher for matters of the heart.

Pisces (Fish) February 19–March 20

This sensitive lifetime sets you free of human incarnations if you allow your profound intuition and innate spiritual wisdom to guide you. These are your gifts. Whenever you stifle your intuition to fit in, you're off path. Be sure to focus your intense feelings on the highest wisdom. Don't get lost in your sensitivity, or relationships will become too painful. You're always the teacher in the room and shouldn't expect others to see what they're not evolved enough to understand. It's essential to live with an open heart and wrap others in healing love—even when you feel wounded yourself. This is especially true in relationships, where you may often feel unloved. By offering your boundless compassion to your partners and to the world, you transcend the challenges of this lifetime and rise to your full potential.

10

FINDING YOUR RELATIONSHIP NUMBER: HOW DO YOU AND YOUR PARTNER ADD UP?

ONCE YOU UNDERSTAND WHAT the numbers reveal, you'll probably figure out the birth paths of everyone you know—especially your family and previous partners. You'll notice that every relationship has its own unique flavor and that you've been drawn to have relationships with some birth paths more than others. You begin to see how your path carries a certain intention that meshes better with partners on a complementary path.

When you add your birth path number to the birth path number of the person you're in a relationship with, you arrive at a number that reveals the flavor of that partnership. It reveals the karma (both good and bad) of your union.

For example, my path is a 22/4 and my husband Gene's path is a 7. The sum of our paths equals 11—a sacred master soul number of healing and inspiration. That number reveals our great gifts and what we're here to do together as well as our challenges.

Gene is my best friend and a huge supporter of my intuition, spiritual wisdom, and career. We share our insights with each other daily, often finishing each other's sentences and usually knowing what the other is thinking. That strong connection is the great gift of our bond.

Our challenge is the downside of the number 11 (the sum of our two path numbers). We're both intuitive and sensitive and know what the other is thinking. So we're capable of hurting one another's feelings without saying a word.

Take your birth path number and add it to the person you're dating or in a relationship with. Example:

Your birth path: 7
Your partner's birth path: 3
Total: 10
Reduced to a single digit: 1
Your relationship number: 1

EVALUATE THE SUM OF YOUR RELATIONSHIP NUMBER

If your relationship sum is 1: You'll both be empowered to own your truth and find your voice through this partnership. There will be enough space between you for each of you to grow and evolve independently. The challenge will be creating intimacy and truly connecting with one another. Instead, you may feel lonely and disconnected even though you're very happy in your own skin.

If your relationship sum is 2: Your challenge and your gift will be connecting deeply with each other. This will be the downfall or the salvation of your union. You're both very sensitive and intuitive and can be hurt easily. Once you move beyond the hurt to open your hearts to each other, you'll bond at such a deep level that you'll carry the other one in your heart every day.

If your relationship sum is 11: You'll have a powerful intuitive spiritual connection that you'll notice from day one. Together you'll create a healing business or platform to do your great work together.

Your challenge will be the intense sensitivity that allows you to know each other's thoughts for better or worse. This requires honesty and shared positive thinking. If you're both spiritually evolved and focus your thoughts on love and gratitude, this could be a mystical union.

If your relationship sum is 3: You'll have a great time together being social, creative, and brilliant. Your parties will be the most fun and your home will be luscious. Your friends will love you and you'll have trouble getting them to leave. Your brilliance will bounce off the walls and you'll enjoy many creative projects together. The problem will be moving from your heads (where you prefer to live) into your hearts and souls. Once you master this and learn to open your hearts to each other, to have feelings, you'll have a wonderful relationship.

If your relationship sum is 4: You can both be stubborn, strong, and willful. It will take a little work to open your hearts and connect. Sharing physical sports and outdoor adventures will bond you. You may decide to run a business together, and your daily dialogue will likely be about your business rather than your feelings. This relationship will probably need weekly therapy or at least family meetings to keep all the parts in working order.

If your relationship sum is 22: You have huge work to share with the world through your partnership. You'll love being inspired together, taking classes, sharing books. You'll want friends who are spiritually inclined and open to new ideas. Together you have a responsibility to teach what you've learned through your powerful, shared career.

If your relationship sum is 5: You have a passionate, sensual connection and love sharing food, music, and travel. This could be a life of pleasure and passion if you're both spiritually strong and aren't tempted by addictions or infidelity. At your best, the two of you will lead a life of fun and travel. You may share a successful business in the natural health or adventure industries. At your worst, you'll lose your way with addictions, jealousy, and self-indulgences.

If your relationship sum is 6: There's possibility for deep, lasting love in this partnership. You'll have a warm, loving home and family that will be hugely important to both of you. But you each must remember who you are and spend some time apart. Otherwise, you risk losing your essential selves and forgetting your own missions and careers.

If your relationship sum is 33: You have a mystical connection—so mystical that you might not be able to make it work in everyday life. Being practical and getting bills paid will be the challenge. You share enormous artistic gifts and could create a project together that uplifts the world. Your shared true work will ultimately have a healing focus. Doing spiritual practices together is essential for your sanity and fulfillment.

If your relationship sum is 7: Your beautiful home will be refined, pristine, and elegant. You'll enjoy exploring spirituality and the arts together. You'll have a powerful intellectual connection and spend many hours analyzing life together. Don't let perfectionism destroy your love, though. You'll intuitively feel each other's energy and may sometimes be wounded by this powerful connection. Opening your hearts to share true warmth and intimacy will be the challenge.

If your relationship sum is 8: Power will be the game you play with each other—for better or worse. Your passion and sexuality will be so powerful it may take you out of the bounds of convention and into dangerous territory. Yet you'll support each other's work and create true abundance together. The question will be: is it true love or is it passion and power?

If your relationship sum is 9: Surrender everything and let the divine energy within you direct this one. You can't control it and you can't walk away from it. The revelations you get from this partnership will be the highest lessons of your lifetime. You'll someday find yourselves holding council for others who want to know how you've made love last. Your answer will be: surrender with love.

IS MY PERFECT PARTNER ON THE
SAME PATH AS I AM?

If you're a 1 path and you fall in love with another 1 path, there are advantages and disadvantages. Here's an overview of how souls on the same paths get along:

1 PATH AND 1 PATH = 2
Each of you will need lots of space and independence and can provide them for your partner. You'll be more comfortable living parallel lives as best friends on a shared journey. True intimacy and chemistry may be lacking, but there's potential for deep respect and understanding between you. You intuit each other's inner motivations, so you'll make a great team. Give each other enough independence, and this partnership could be a fulfilling and lasting one.

2 PATH AND 2 PATH = 4
You both crave intimacy, and you'll be intuitively connected from the day you meet. You'll have organized, clean homes and love working together. You'll probably want to spend all your time together. But your deep sensitivity means you'll both keep getting your feelings hurt and there will be lots of drama. You'll have to work every day to clear up miscommunications and nurture each other's sensitivity.

3 PATH AND 3 PATH = 6
There's plenty of fun and creativity in this relationship, and you'll eventually long to start a family. But who's going to make a living? At your best, you'll create a business to share and make it successful with your creative ideas. You may argue about who runs the busi-

ness and who gets to stay home with the kids. At your worst, you'll both be stuck in your heads with little emotional warmth between you. Yet the potential is here to help each other open up and heal many old wounds from the past while you create a loving home and family.

4 PATH AND 4 PATH = 8

Lots of work gets done in this partnership, and you'll both love exercising, hiking, and keeping fit. Your combined hard work will create great financial success. But beware of burying yourselves in the day-to-day drudgery. You may end up spending little time together because of your shared work addiction—unless you work together. Because you're both so strong, you need help opening your hearts to each other. One of you will have to initiate relaxation, vacations, and love dates. Money and success will thrive in your partnership as long as you both do the work required and neither of you tries to control the other.

5 PATH AND 5 PATH = 1

You share great sensuality and a passionate love of food, music, sex, and adventure. But you'll each be tempted to go your own way. Fidelity will be an issue, so please don't allow drugs or alcohol in the house, or addictions may destroy your great chemistry. If you immerse yourselves in spirituality and your independent careers, you can have a lasting love. Your challenge will be pulling yourselves away from indulgences and the temptations of others. Focusing on healthy living and a daily meditation practice will save you.

6 PATH AND 6 PATH = 3

Family and home will be your primary focus, but if you can both launch careers as healers or artists, this could work. Be careful not to lose yourselves in each other or in the kids. Personal growth and a strong spiritual practice will keep you and your family happy and healthy. Your shared creativity will spark plenty of brilliant new ideas such as artistic projects, home design and remodeling, and healthy gourmet cooking.

7 PATH AND 7 PATH = 5

Picture Einstein discussing quantum physics with Niels Bohr and you get the picture of what's possible here: two brilliant minds analyzing the world together. But unless one of you opens your heart, this relationship could be a cold one. You'll agree on lots of things, love the same hobbies, and want the same peaceful, elegant living space. But getting out of your heads will be the challenge. Once you learn to quiet your minds, enormous physical passion is possible. And if you each embrace spirituality and intuition, your passion will take on an otherworldly connection that will feed your soul.

8 PATH AND 8 PATH = 7

Unless you're highly evolved, this could be an abusive power struggle as you battle each other for control. If you're spiritually conscious beings and you've already owned your power in the world, this enlightened partnership can result in huge success and joint philanthropic endeavors. But you'll need lots of space between you to reduce the competitive friction. Respecting and empowering each other to do big work is essential for happiness. Exploring and practicing daily spiritual exercises, such as meditation or prayer, is required to make this partnership thrive and prosper.

9 PATH AND 9 PATH = 9

You're two wise old souls joining hands to save the world. You have deep simpatico and a shared wisdom from lifetimes of challenges and successes. Humanitarian work is essential for both of you. Launch a nonprofit foundation together or become Science of the Mind ministers. It's essential that you both embrace your spirituality and step away from disappointments and past losses. If you can do this, the wisdom and love you share will be deeply fulfilling, but there will be lots of surrender required to make the relationship work.

11 PATH AND 11 PATH = 22/4

The intensity of your sensitivities and the high frequency of your energy will generate great sparks and passion, but this relationship must help both of you use your gifts to change the world. If not, you may end up destroying each other with your high-voltage energy. If you're both spiritually evolved, you could create a partnership of twin souls reaching for the highest light in shared work and love.

22 PATH AND 22 PATH = 8

Let's change the world together and generate enormous abundance for everyone! That seems to be the agreement here. Imagine a household with two Oprahs or two Donald Trumps. Who's going to answer the phone? You will have so much important work to get done that you'll definitely need to hire a cook and housekeeper. Your brilliant ideas and inspiring conversations will flow endlessly through the day and into the night. Fascinating, high-powered friends will fill your dinner table. You won't have patience for trivia or fools. If you do your great work together, you will change the world and become one of the wealthiest couples in the world.

33 PATH AND 33 PATH = 3

This connection will at first feel energized and fun—but I caution against it. There's a distinct possibility of both of you becoming untethered from reality, a shift precipitated by drugs, alcohol, or spiritual practices. Your creativity and artistic gifts are enormous. Someone has to keep your feet on the ground. Who will feed you and pay the bills? You're the great explorers of the unknown realms, but you must also bring that knowledge back to planet Earth in a healing way—and that takes work. If you're both deeply immersed in powerful spiritual work, this relationship could work. You can be shamans, saints, and artists who, together, heal the world.

11

DECIPHERING YOUR SOUL-MATE AGREEMENT

LOOKING BACK AT YOUR past, you've probably recognized repeated cycles of beginnings and endings, deaths and rebirths—
all similar to the seasons of growth found in the natural world.
There were times of great excitement when you fell in love, got a
new job, or moved to a better location. At other times, you faced
challenges such as heartbreak, disappointment, or a health crisis.

Are these cycles on purpose? Is there an order to how your life
and lessons have unfolded? Is there a way to see these changes coming? Is it possible to live in the flow of grace, knowing exactly how to
handle every crisis and opportunity?

According to Pythagoras's theory of numbers, the answer is yes!

Every year of your life, says Pythagoras, you've been under the
vibrational influence of a particular number—1 through 9 or 11, 22,
or 33—within a repeating nine-year cycle. After each nine-year cycle
is complete, a new one begins, bringing the benefits and burdens of
the last cycle into the new one.

You planned this, of course. You realized you would need
many opportunities to evolve your soul and accomplish your mission. You recognized that you would learn certain lessons at certain times in your life when you would be best equipped to make
the changes required. You made agreements with your soul mates

about when they could enter or exit your life; you created the schedule that would best suit your evolution. You signed up for this timetable and outlined the agenda for your life's turning points!

Let's determine where you are in that nine-year cycle and how it has been affecting your relationships.

PERSONAL-YEAR CYCLES

You began this lifetime under the influence of the birth path number you chose. If that number is 3, then the first year of your life was a 3 personal year. The second year of your life was a 4 personal year, and so on.

Your current personal year is determined by the single-digit numbers of your birth month and birth date added to the current calendar year and reduced to a single digit or master number.

Here is an example of personal-year calculation:

BIRTH DATE: SEPTEMBER 15, 1951

Month: Sept=9
Date: 15=6
Current Year: 2012=5
9+6+5=20=2
Personal year: 2

CALCULATE YOUR PERSONAL YEAR:

Your birth month: _____

Your birth date: _____

Current year: _____

Total: _____

Reduced to a single digit: _____

This is your personal year: _____

MEANING OF THE PERSONAL YEARS

PERSONAL YEAR 1

Relationships may spark your interest or tempt you into romance, but just say no. If love is meant to be, it will still be there next year when you're ready. You'll have lots of new people coming into your life this year. But it's a year to focus on YOU—and not on relationships. It's time to launch your business, get a new job or title, start a graduate program, or move to a new location. Everything you do this year will influence the events of your life for the next nine years. If you don't plant seeds for a better future now, nothing will come to bloom as this cycle unfolds. Tap into all the new energy that will help you release the past and reinvent. There's never been a better time for taking steps toward your ultimate dream. Everything revolves around you and is dependent on you. Believe in your vision, make important decisions alone, and move forward bravely—like a pioneer.

PERSONAL YEAR 2

This is your year for connecting deeply with someone—but only if you've released the past and realigned your direction. Your career won't be all on your shoulders anymore as others step forward to offer support for the project you started last year. It's a slower, sweeter year, one in which you nurture what you've already started rather than pushing hard to launch new things. Success hinges on opening your heart, trusting your heightened intuition, and saying yes to collaboration. It's important to be receptive. Soften the forceful energy you thrived on last year. You might feel highly sensitive now, but don't let this get in the way of love. Your solution is to become the source of love for others—even when you're feeling wounded.

PERSONAL YEAR 11

This year is a sacred one for relationships. If you're single, your best-ever partner shows up now. The success of this new relationship hinges on whether you've done your inner work and found your true path. With or without a partner, it's a highly charged year of personal illumination and intellectual achievement. You'll be inspired to heal all the relationships in your life and accomplish your most inspired work. Your intuition, inspiration, and artistic creativity are magnified and so is your sensitivity. Daily meditation or prayer will enhance all of your gifts and reinforce your connection to the divine. That spiritual connection is more powerful than ever this year. Use it as your source for actions. Spend time with highly evolved, conscious people who inspire you to create. Small talk and meaningless social engagements will drain you because of your heightened sensitivity. This is your best year for developing spiritual, intuitive, and artistic gifts as well as for learning to love in a profoundly new way.

PERSONAL YEAR 3

If you started a new relationship last year, this is the fun, sexy, playful year to deepen your communication and get to know each other's friends. It's also time to create projects for your new work. Express yourself, get into the center of things, join social groups, and entertain. Forget long-term planning and just enjoy life; don't make important decisions about your future. Develop your skills with words—written and spoken. Life is your stage—enjoy it! Whatever you started in your 1 year through hard work and diligence is now reaping enjoyment for you. It's a year to blossom.

PERSONAL YEAR 4

If you're single in this 4 year, it's time to focus on your work. Just get it done. Next year's energy will push you back out into the world to find your mate. If you're in a relationship now, this is the year to build your house, so to speak. Focus on being responsible to your partner and career, combining your lives, and tapping into core strengths whenever challenged. It's a serious year to fulfill obligations, get practical and organized, and build the foundation for future growth. Create your budget and do the physical work. Get your home in order—whether that means moving, remodeling, or cleaning. Get in shape physically and cultivate strength in all areas of life. Dependability, honesty, and responsibility are required in relationship and career.

PERSONAL YEAR 22

This is your best year for manifesting inspired work in the world. Anything is possible! If you're in a relationship, harness your partner's help to accomplish all that's on your plate. Ignoring your work will leave you feeling off-balance, unfocused, and useless. Use inspiration as your fuel to get it all done. If you're single, don't waste a moment looking for love or going on long vacations (you won't be able to relax). Focus on your great work and trust that love and relaxation will come later. This is a year for putting personal concerns aside and doing your best for the world at large. Make big plans and introduce changes. You'll have the opportunity to ascend to your greatest career achievements and acquire abundant financial rewards. You'll also feel the sting of criticism that greatness attracts. Focus on your work and keep moving forward.

PERSONAL YEAR 5

This year, sparks of attraction will fly with everyone you meet. Your charisma is amped up and your magnetism is attracting everyone—from potential partners to new business opportunities. You're as potent as a cat in heat! Hold steady to your true self or you'll get pulled off path by every suitor. Instead, wait for the right one—the partner you've seen and felt intuitively in your dreams. Be open, fearless, passionate, and free, and your soul mate will show up beside you. You'll have opportunities for expansion, adventure, and the unexpected in this turning-point year. Everything is vibrant and changing around you. Take trips (it's time for that long vacation), investigate career opportunities, and get rid of anything or anyone monotonous or boring. Eliminate conditions and people that hold you back. Make room for the new. Focus on freedom and adapting to change. Enjoy this sensual year with good food, new relationships, and trips to exotic places. You'll be supercharged, attractive, and sexual. You can revive tedious relationships or work circumstances with your new energy and charisma.

PERSONAL YEAR 6

This year is a time of deep love and nurturing. Focus on marriage, commitment, family, and responsibility. Your heart opens wide to embrace your partner. If you're single and someone new dances into your life, say yes. It's time to either fall in love or deepen your commitment to the one already at your side. Rather than focus on yourself, adjust to the needs of others. Enjoy couple and family activities as you shift away from the passionate excesses of the 5 personal year. Marriage and close friendships will blossom as you nurture them with your new openhearted energy. Reach out to understand the people in your life. Let go of superficiality and take responsibility for others. Yet don't take on more than you can carry, or you'll fall into depression and be overwhelmed. This is one year, though, when general harmony is more important than your own needs.

PERSONAL YEAR 33

You'll be drawn to mystical knowledge, intuition, and spiritual guidance this year. But if you're not grounded, you could become disconnected to everyday reality. Stay away from alcohol and drugs and meditate every day. If you embrace your higher self, it will be your most inspired year artistically. You'll channel in genius—whether you're an actor, musician, or artist. Your pipeline to the divine is opened up and flowing freely with spiritual and creative inspiration. Take a meditation retreat and create, create, create! Your finished product and enlightened ideas will change the world.

PERSONAL YEAR 7

This is not a party year. It's time for deep reflection, intuitive development, and spiritual growth. If you're already in a relationship, take your partner's hand and bring him on the inner journey with you. Sign up for a meditation and yoga retreat together. If you're single, deepen your connection with spirit. Take meditation classes and spend a weekend in prayer and silence. Strength will only come from your connection to the divine. You may feel a bit lonely or isolated, whether you're in a relationship or not. Use your alone time to write a book, research higher consciousness, or take a psychology class. Focus on finding your true purpose. Withdraw from the center of things; superficial social events won't feel good. Your sensitivity and intuition are elevated, and you'll pick up other people's feelings everywhere you go. Refine what you started in this nine-year cycle by analyzing and perfecting projects and relationships. Your intuition will be at its most powerful—rely on it for all decisions. Pursue nothing—you'll naturally attract what is meant to be in your life.

PERSONAL YEAR 8

If you're already in a relationship, money and career will be the topic of nearly every conversation. If you're single, you may meet your new partner through business connections. But you'll have many opportunities to make money and advance your career, and those should be your focus. It's a year to go to the bank—not the bar. Even when you go out partying, your mind will be home crunching numbers to see how you can improve your business or pay off your debts. It's time to own your power both financially and physically. Get back into shape—financially and physically. If you wrote a book last year, this is the year to promote and sell it. If you researched and developed your new business last year, now is the time to get it funded. Physical accomplishment and material success are your focus, as you reap the seeds of success that you planted early in this nine-year cycle. During this powerful year, take command to get results. Think big, manage and direct others, move forward. Beware of abusing your power in relationships or becoming greedy with your partner. Be patient and generous to others—even if that feels tedious.

PERSONAL YEAR 9

If you're single, don't look for a new partner this year. You won't start a lasting relationship while wrapping up this nine-year cycle. You might bring in a new love who teaches you an important lesson for this lifetime. But it's not a year for lasting love. If you're married, you may consider ending your marriage. You'll review all the shortcomings of your partner and see clearly what needs to be fixed. If you choose to bring the partner into your next cycle, you'll have to heal and reinvent the marriage. Friends and lovers from the past will resurface to be examined, then kept or discarded for the next cycle. Your career will conclude the focus that it has had for the past nine years, even though you won't see the new cycle just yet. Open your hands and let go, with faith that something new and better will arrive in your 1 year. You may even be fired or laid off. Relationships will fall away or be transformed, and you'll grieve for your losses over the past nine years. Peace comes from higher wisdom and a greater connection to spirituality. Your insights and wisdom will be heightened. Use this awareness to benefit the people around you. Focus on artistic and spiritual disciplines, and wait for the new inspiration that begins soon in your approaching 1 year.

MORE TRANSITION POINTS:
THE GROWTH OPPORTUNITIES IN YOUR
TWO SATURN RETURNINGS

At the ages of twenty-eight and twenty-nine, you'll experience your first Saturn returning. This is a major transition point and your first true wake-up call. Events will transpire to show you clearly what you're here to do in this lifetime. You'll see a new vision of who you are—as opposed to what you imagined while growing up and what's been expected of you. You'll finally walk away from family and friends who've held you back. This time is often one of broken relationships, heartbreak, and career change—all perfectly designed to move you forward and release the past. If your soul needs powerful fuel to accomplish your mission, you may experience revelations and possibly trauma at this age. This trauma will pinpoint exactly what you're here to do—even if you're not able to begin that great work until later in life. Someday you'll look back at this time and say, "Thank goodness that happened or I wouldn't be here now doing what I love and having such a fulfilling career and relationship." Below is a story to help you see the significance of this transition time.

YOUR FIRST SATURN RETURNING

It's a clear-blue-sky Colorado day, and we're sitting on the secret rock outcropping hidden from the well-traveled trail where we spent the morning hiking. The hike has left us sweaty and tired, but the view in front of us is stunning—a majestic spread of snow-capped mountains. Mist rises from the valleys at our feet. Our backs rest against the warm, sun-drenched granite slabs. "I'm sorry about your relationship ending," I say as we share dried fruit and chocolate.

"It hadn't felt right for a long time." You sigh, looking out over the horizon. "We were planning to get married. But it wouldn't have worked." You wipe a tear from your cheek and look away down the valley.

"What will you do now?" I ask.

"I don't know if I'm capable of a lasting relationship," you whisper. "Don't think it's in my genes. My parents' marriage was a disaster."

"Your parents are part of a soul agreement you made long ago. They were showing you something you wanted to change about yourself. You might be married now in an impossible relationship if it weren't for watching your parents and deciding you wanted something better. This is your gift from them," I explain. "It means you want to break an old negative pattern in yourself."

You turn and look directly at me while taking the water bottle from my hand. There's a long pause. "OK, I've never looked at it that way."

A huge black crow with an enormous wingspan lands on a rock to our right. The majestic bird stares directly at us and begins cawing loudly—as if he's trying to tell us something. We both look at each other and giggle. "What's he saying?" you ask.

"He wants you to pay attention. He's telling you that you have a huge soul mission and this painful time is helping you reinvent so you can accomplish it." The crow spreads his wings and lifts off the rock, swooping down across the valley in front of us.

You take a long drink from the water bottle. "Did I tell you that I think I'm getting laid off at work?"

"Congratulations. Your complete reinvention is under way."

"I don't understand anything about my life anymore—where I'm headed or what I'm supposed to do now. I thought I had it all figured out. I'm twenty-eight years old and everything has fallen apart. It's like I don't know whose life I've been living." You look into the distance at the mountain peaks and the shimmering sky above them. We're both quiet.

"I think you know everything," I whisper. "I think you know

exactly what you want your life to look like and you're afraid to own it because it feels too big and impossible."

You lean back and take a long deep breath, closing your eyes and resting your head against the warm granite rock behind us. "Truth is, I've hated my job for a while, and that didn't help my relationship. I usually came home in a bad mood. I never felt passionate about that career. I chose it for financial security."

"Did it give you financial security?"

"I'm completely broke," you mumble.

"Whenever we take a job for security, it never brings us money or happiness if it's not our true work. We can only create abundance from doing what we came here to do."

"So *now* you tell me," you say with a smile, leaning back against the rock, eyes closed.

"Do you remember when you were in high school and made films? Do you remember how much you loved doing that? Remember that awesome documentary you made for your senior project? Your teachers loved it. You won an award for it."

You turn and face me. "That's painful to think about," you whisper. "I loved it, but I didn't believe I could be successful at that. How many people do you know who get to make movies for their living?"

You pick up a pebble in the dirt beside you and throw it forcefully into the space in front of us. It soars and disappears down into the green valley at our feet. "My parents didn't encourage me. They said there were too many unemployed filmmakers in the world and they wouldn't pay for me to study that at college."

"Another piece of your soul-mate agreement with them," I say gently, "a moment when you could have owned your power and stood up for your dream anyway."

You look away and draw a circle in the dry dust beside your feet.

"None of those unemployed filmmakers are YOU," I say quietly.

"What do you mean?"

"You had a gift for it. Everyone told you that. It lit you up! You wanted to travel to Africa and film a documentary about the children who've lost their parents to AIDS. One of your teachers showed you how to apply for a grant to do that."

"Instead I went to college to study marketing. That's what my parents paid for."

"Oh right, the practical degree that got you the secure job that you hated and are now losing."

"Yeah." You smile. You close your eyes again, leaning back against the warm rock. I look over and see the slight smile on your face. You're quiet for quite a while until you say, "Did I tell you I shot a little film recently about a boy who . . ."

As you begin talking about filmmaking, your voice becomes more animated. An hour of lively conversation passes quickly as the sun moves across the sky. We discuss the classes you want to take, the new camera you bought recently, and the film workshop you almost signed up for. We come up with ideas for funding your documentary. You get more and more excited.

After a while you pause and say: "But who do I think I am to believe I could make a living from making films?"

"Who do you think you are to ignore the gifts you brought in and the mission you came to accomplish?" I answer. "Divine order is waiting for you to take a step forward. After that, doors open and magic happens to make you successful because it's your true work."

"You've really seen this work for other people?"

"I see it unfold every day in my clients' lives. It's your true path, and when you meet your soul mate, you're introducing yourself as a filmmaker—not as a grumpy marketing executive."

You look at me and smile. By the time we start hiking down the trail toward home, you're laughing and there's energy in your steps.

YOUR SECOND SATURN RETURNING
At the ages of fifty-eight and fifty-nine, you go through your second Saturn returning—the second major transition point of your life-

time. It's designed to strip you of any worldly pretense or false defi-nitions of self that you've accumulated through your career. Your authentic gift is all that remains after you've completed these power-ful two years.

If you've been identifying yourself as a brilliant software engi-neer, yet you're here to share your creative visions through books or film, your software career will come to an abrupt end. If you've been hiding out in a relationship that did not support your true self in the world, that relationship will crumble.

The heat is turned up for transformation in every area of your life, from career to love and health. Your soul is saying, "It's now or never and you wanted to get this done. Wake up!"

Events will occur that leave you feeling stripped naked in the world. Only your true self will remain. All of these changes will help you become your most honest, daring self in the world. It's time to be completely authentic in your greatest work. The universe will not allow you to play it small or give yourself away.

And if you've already been traveling the right path, it's time to kick it up a notch!

Here's a story:

"How can I possibly start over?" you ask as we stare at the waves tumbling toward us on the beach. "I'm older now. Who would hire me?"

"It's better this way," I whisper. "You know it wasn't good the way it was."

"Yes, I know that."

"Do you remember being happy?" I ask as we watch a flock of gulls squawking overhead on their way out to sea.

"Yes, it was in the early days of my career. I felt filled with pos-sibility. But my job became mostly drudgery and politics. None of that had anything to do with why I started."

"Who were you back then?" I ask. "What did you want your career to look like?"

"I wanted to BE somebody—somebody smart and innovative who inspired people, somebody who made a difference."

"It didn't turn out that way, did it? Why did you stay?"

"Money and benefits. I was raising a family and afraid to give up job security. Now I'm tired from all the drama. I don't have the energy to start over. Yet I still have to make a living. I'm applying to jobs that I care nothing about and NOT getting interviews."

"You signed up for this challenge. Don't bail out now. You chose to be here in the midst of this economic crisis to be forced to remember your real mission: to raise the consciousness of the planet with your gifts and talents—through your work," I remind you as we walk across the warm sand.

"It seems that everything is about money now," you say with frustration in your voice. "Everyone is making choices because of money—not because of who they are inside or their mission."

"We're looking at this exactly backward," I explain. "Right now we're being called to do our great work—every one of us. We need to focus on the new and enlightened ideas that inspire us. When we grab hold of those ideas and launch a business or create a technology or think in a new way to solve an old problem, then money flows effortlessly."

"So you're saying I'm stuck in the past."

"Your pattern of looking at career as simply a paycheck and benefits is an old paradigm that's crumbling right now. It's up for reinvention, thank goodness." I laugh and sit on the warm sand. "When we think in those old patterns about work and money, we buy into the scarcity mind-set that's paralyzing so many people. There's still plenty of abundance on this planet. We're required now to work in more conscious, inspired ways to attract it."

"How would I do that?" you ask with softness coming back into your voice as you sit on the sand beside me.

"You take all the knowledge and experience you gained in your old career and wrap it all together in a different way—a way that's in alignment with who you are, with your path, and why you came here."

"How?" you ask after a long pause, running your fingers through the white sand.

"Remember when we talked about your path being one of enlightenment—bringing new ideas to the world to solve our everyday problems?"

"That's a far cry from what I've been doing for a paycheck."

"That's why it didn't work out for you. You weren't living up to your true potential—what you signed up to do."

"But how does someone make a living and support a family doing THAT? I told you my wife divorced me and I have to pay child support, alimony, and college tuition."

"Our true work, the work we came here to do, always DOES support us financially. It's the only real path to abundance and success. And you have to be doing your true work to attract your soul mate. That's the law of divine order."

"If this is all governed by divine order, why is there such suffering and chaos? Why am I so confused?"

"This world and its illusions provide the resistance required to help us find our strength and purpose, to remember who we are. In other words, it's a great workout for the soul."

"I was so unhappy in my job. I know it played a big role in my marriage ending. I want to be the happy good guy I was when I started out." You look up at the white billowing clouds on the horizon and take a deep breath. "You know, for years I've dreamt of using my engineering background to develop a new technology that combines wind and solar. I keep thinking about that."

"Well, that's your intuition, your higher self, telling you that's what you came here to do."

"The funny thing is that in college I was part of a team that developed technology that enabled physically challenged people to work on computers. I used my engineering talent to create something inspired and meaningful. It's like I knew back then. And then I fell off path."

"You chose survival instead of pursuing your dream. It's the same choice nearly everyone makes. But we're experiencing a shift of consciousness now—an opening. What if you could become the person you dreamt of being long ago?"

"How would I go about getting my idea going and making money from it?" you ask as we stand up and start walking toward home.

"Now you're talking." I laugh, brushing the sand from my clothes. "When we get back, we'll make a list of action steps. And by the way, once you take a few steps in this new direction, your new soul mate will show up. You're introducing yourself to her as the CEO of a new alternative energy company."

"That feels right," you say, taking a deep breath and smiling. "That feels right . . ."

TOBI'S STORY: A REAL STORY OF REINVENTION

Tobi majored in speech and communications in college, but she never really had a chance to launch her career. She got married at the age of twenty-three and had two children soon afterward. As a Pisces 11-path soul, she had always focused on relationships more than career success, so being a full-time mom fulfilled her in every way.

She was happy to let her career take a back burner. For a few years, it worked well. Eventually she realized that it wasn't the life she'd imagined. She had no income of her own and her husband was always working. He didn't appreciate Tobi's intuitive, sensitive nature. This disconnect caused great stress in the family and left Tobi feeling powerless and insecure.

When the children were nine and five years old, her ten-year marriage ended. This event coincided perfectly with Tobi's 9 personal year, marking the end of a major cycle in her life.

"My primary goal then was to be the best single mom that I could be and support my children the best way that I knew how. I didn't have many skills when I reentered the workforce after years of being home with the children," she remembers. "I didn't feel confident in myself, especially having lived with a verbally abusive husband for over fifteen years."

Tobi took a small job sorting mail and answering phones for a financial company. She worked her way up the ladder, mastering computer knowledge and sales skills until she landed a better job selling insurance products. "My passion was not working in the insurance industry, but I liked dealing with most of the customers. It was a way to earn a meager living, pay the bills, and support my children."

In 2003, a large financial company hired her as a "relationship manager," which was much more challenging because of its substantial sales goals. But Tobi's gift was connecting with people, so this job fit her very well and helped her gain confidence.

"But I soon became very disenchanted with the management style of my bosses. It was hard to work in that negativity and still be motivated to succeed. But I did, and I won many performance awards over the next seven years," she recalls.

Because connecting with people made her happy, Tobi joined several local women's networking groups. "I loved meeting the brilliant, supportive women who belonged to the groups. But my job grew more and more miserable."

To forge more relationships in the community, she became the programming vice president for a well-known national women's networking group and was responsible for booking speakers and creating events for the monthly meetings. "That position came very easily to me, and I quickly won an award for the best programs in the state. I was beginning to understand my strengths and who I was."

Her bank job was still her primary source of income, and it was causing increasing stress in her life. To bring in extra money, she started her own networking group, which boasted fifty to eighty attendees each month.

Yet this networking group was not her full focus, and she devoted most of her hours to her full-time bank job. "The relationships coming out of these networking meetings were astonishing and so rewarding, but still most of my focus went to surviving at my job. I felt torn between my passion for connecting with others and my need to make a secure income."

In 2009, Tobi came to me for an intuitive reading and learned about her master-soul path of the 11—to create healing and deep connection with others, inspiring others to fulfill their potential. "It was one of the best days of my life. I felt so affirmed and happy. It really changed my life," she says.

This new perspective on her life explained why she was so passionate about creating networking events to bring people together for inspiration and connection. Yet how could she make a career change and also support her family?

"I knew I had to leave the bank, but I was too afraid to give up the salary, security, and benefits."

During our session, we discussed Tobi's 9 personal year fast approaching in 2010 and how it probably meant the bank job was finished one way or the other.

"I lost my job in my 9 personal year. Deep down, I was thrilled. If I didn't have Sue's words to fall back on and my mission in life, I would have fallen apart. But I knew that this is what was needed for me to fulfill my soul's purpose."

Today, Tobi is a full-time event planner and loves what she does. "I'm organizing a huge women's expo this June with eighty-five-plus vendor booths with eight amazing, empowering speakers and inspirational content. I use my network meetings to raise money for local nonprofit organizations that benefit mental health issues and a women's shelter. I run a monthly networking luncheon and monthly breakfast and dinner groups, too. I love my life now, am making good money, and can't wait to see how it all unfolds!"

Tobi believes that if her first marriage had not ended so painfully she would never have found her true gifts in the world. "I would probably have hidden out as a wife and mother and not recognized the bigger work I was here to do."

During her years of stepping up to her power and true work, she found the most loving partner she's ever had, and today he shares her life and work. Steve is a Taurus 33 path and truly embraces her spiritual perspective on life. "We are truly blessed in our relationship, and he understands and supports me more than anyone ever has. But I had to find ME first before he could find and love me. He has been better to me than my first husband ever was."

Here's Tobi's story of meeting her soul mate:

"I have to tell you that I did not love him when I first met him. He didn't fit the image of the young, sexy man I thought I wanted in my life. In fact, we were just friends for about a year before anything sexual happened. It was the first time that I was really good friends with a man before a more intimate relationship occurred. We would go out to dinner often and talk and talk. We also did ballroom dancing, which was such fun, and I would go out singing karaoke. Steve loved my singing voice.

"We met on a March 19. This is a really weird thing because my first marriage broke up on a March 19. I met Steve at a ladies' night out at a local hotel on a Wednesday night. When my friend Jackie saw me talking to Steve, at the end of the night, she pulled me away from him, saying that he had white hair and was too old for me.

"I only spoke to Steve for about five to ten minutes that first night and then left. I never knew his name, but I remember saying to him that he looked like a movie star! I was thinking about an old-time Hollywood star named Jeff Chandler. Steve reminded me of him.

"We ran into each other four days later in the local supermarket and started talking. He said he was going on a business trip and would call me when he returned—but he never did. Finally, the following week, he called me at work and said that he, his boss, and business partner were all involved in a very serious car accident in Pittsburgh and that he should have been killed. He felt God had spared his life for a reason, and he asked me out.

"He said he hadn't had a date for years and asked me to be gentle with him. I remember saying, 'Just feed me and you'll be fine.' That was several pounds ago! (We still love to eat out.) But I think things changed when I introduced Steve to my daughter Jolie, who told me after meeting him that she loved him and that I shouldn't screw up the relationship. I listened to her and felt that he was better for me than the young men I had dated in the past.

"We've known each other several years now and have been through so much together. But as the years go by, I love and respect him more each day. He's a wonderful man with such great values and so much integrity. He loves me more than ever, too. Steve really supports me in whatever I do. He always stands up for me and will do anything to help me, including ironing my clothes, cooking, and driving me to meetings or networking events. What a gem! I couldn't be doing what I do now without his love and encouragement."

12

WORKBOOK FOR SEEING YOUR PATH AND SOUL AGREEMENTS

YOUR DETAILED LIFE MISSION and soul-mate agreements are encoded into your name and your date of birth—which can be reduced to a simple numerological code first identified by Pythagoras.

In his system, every number from 1 through 9 has a positive and negative vibration (which shows its potential and its challenges). Your destiny number—derived from your birth date—is a picture of the mission you came here to achieve, along with the potential pitfalls of your path. By understanding this number, you can make wise choices for you career and love life.

In numerology, all numbers are reduced to the digits 1 through 9, except for three cosmic vibrations symbolized by the master numbers 11, 22, and 33. All other numbers are reduced to the basic digits 1 through 9 by adding the digits of the entire number together.

For example, the number 43 equals 7 (4+3=7), and 10 equals 1 (1+0=1).

Every letter of the alphabet also corresponds to the numbers 1 through 9. For example, A=1, B=2, C=3, and so on.

In your birth path calculations, reduce all numbers down to a single digit, except for the master numbers 11, 22, and 33, which in your final calculations only stay as 11/2, 22/4, and 33/6.

EXAMPLE OF BIRTH PATH CALCULATION

> Birth date: October 16, 1980
> Month=October equals 10, equals 1 (1+0=1)
> Date=16 equals 7 (1+6=7)
> Year=1980 equals 9
> 9=(1+9+8+0=18) (1+8=9)
> Total of month (1) plus date (7) plus year (9) equals 17, which
>   equals 8 (8=1+7)
> Birth path=8 (1+7+9=17=8)

THE MASTER SOUL NUMBERS

The master numbers of 11, 22, and 33 represent sacred birth paths designed to help humanity evolve. Those numbers are not reduced to a single digit in the final birth path calculations. (But they are reduced to single digits when calculating your final sum. For example, the month of November digits down to a 2 to determine your birth path number.)

EXAMPLE OF A MASTER SOUL BIRTH PATH CALCULATION

> Birth date: September 15, 1951
> Month=September equals 9
> Date=15 equals 6 (1+5=6)
> Year=1951 equals 7
> 7=(1+9+5+1=16) (1+6)
> Total of month (9) plus date (6) plus year
>   (7) equals 22
> Total=22 master path soul (9+6+7=22)

This is also referred to as a 22/4 path since the 22 is always connected to the 4 path. Similarly, the 11 path is referred to as 11/2 path, and the 33 path is referred to as a 33/6 path.

THREE WAYS OF ADDING BIRTH DATES

It's important to add each birth date three different ways to check your addition and to look for hidden master path numbers.

This is especially important if you've arrived at a 2, 4, or 6 birth path calculation. These birth paths often contain a hidden 11, 22, or 33 path if added two other ways. If the master soul number is "hidden" in this way, it means this person will choose when they're ready to step up to their great work—usually later in life.

EXAMPLES

These are the three ways you would add this birth date to discover that two out of three ways reveal a 22/4 path while the third way reveals a 13/4.

BIRTH DATE: MAY 1, 1960 = 22/4 PATH		
FIRST (TRADITIONAL) METHOD	SECOND METHOD	THIRD METHOD
May = 5	5	5+1+1+9+6+0=22/4
1 = 1	1	
1960 = +7	+1960	
Total = 13 = 4 (3+1=4)	1966 = 22/4	
	(1+9+6+6=22)	

Here is another example of the three methods; this one uses the birth date September 15, 1951.

BIRTH DATE: SEPTEMBER 15, 1951 = 22/4 PATH

FIRST (TRADITIONAL) METHOD	SECOND METHOD	THIRD METHOD
September= 9	1951	9+1+5+1+9+5+1=31
15 = 6	15	=4 (3+1=4)
1951 = +7	+9	
Total = 22	1975=22	
(9+6+7= 22)	(1+9+7+5=22)	

Another example of third method, using President Barack Obama's birth date of August 4, 1961:

$$8+4+1+9+6+1=29=2+9=11$$

His birth path is a hidden 11/2 master soul path, meaning that 11/2 is the final calculation only when added with the third method. The other two methods both result in a final calculation of 20/2. Because it's a "hidden" master soul number it means he chose when he was ready to step up to do his great work. Until then, he could fit easily into conventional careers without revealing his true spiritual essence.

CALCULATE YOUR BIRTH PATH

Use your date of birth to calculate your birth path according to all three of the methods displayed above:

First method result: _____

Second method result: _____

Third method result: _____

All three methods should arrive at the same final number—even if you discover you're on a master soul path of 11, 22, or 33. Those master-soul-path calculations result in the consistent final combinations of 11/2, 22/4, or 33/6—at least one of the ways you add the birth date. The other two ways may result in various other two-digit numbers that when added together total 2, 4, or 6. (Examples are 20/2, 13/4, or 15/6.)

Your birth month: _____

Your birth date: _____

Your birth year: _____

Total: _____

Reduced to a single digit: _____

Your birth path number: _____

EXERCISE

After learning about your birth path number and what it means, do you believe you're doing your great work now? Write your thoughts about how your birth path applies to your career:

_____

How can you tweak your career to line it up more with your birth path? How can you focus more on aligning with your birth path in your career and life so that your soul mate can join you?

_____

_____

_____

_____

In relationships, what other birth paths are most compatible with your path and why?

_____

_____

_____

_____

Which paths are challenging for you and why?

_____

_____

_____

_____

Do you see a pattern of certain birth path types that you've attracted in previous relationships? How's that been working for you?

_____

_____

_____

_____

Which birth paths would you like to bring into your life more through friends and partners? Explain why:

_____

_____

_____

_____

Write three steps you're willing to take to live true to your path so you can fulfill your great potential and attract your soul mate:

_____

_____

_____

_____

YOUR RELATIONSHIP-NUMBER CALCULATION

When you add your birth path number to the birth path number of the person you're in a relationship with, you arrive at a number that reveals the flavor of that partnership. It reveals the karma (both good and bad) of your union. This is your relationship number.

If you're currently (or previously were) dating someone, add that person's birth path number to yours. What's the sum of your and your partner's paths? For example, if you're on a 7 path and your partner is on a 4 path, your relationship number is an 11. This means that your challenges (extreme sensitivity) and your gifts (intuition, deep connection, and inspiration) are all reflected in the number 11, which is a divine number of healing and transformation.

Your birth path: _____

Your partner's birth path: _____

Total: _____

Reduced to a single digit: _____

Your relationship number: _____

EXERCISE

What can you learn from this? Which relationship numbers have been most successful for you in the past? Which relationship numbers have been least successful for you?

_____

_____

_____

_____

Calculate your best friends' birth path and then calculate your shared relationship number. Does this relationship number reveal a pattern that you should look for in someone you date?

_____

_____

_____

_____

When you study the relationship numbers that seem most positive in your life, what can you learn about choosing a partner?

_____

_____

_____

_____

YOUR CURRENT CAREER AND LOVE YEAR

Every year of your life you've been under the influence of a particular number—1 through 9, 11, 22, or 33. Since all of our learning takes place within the vibrational range of these numbers, you're working with a different type of energy each year, within a repeating nine-year cycle.

You started this lifetime in the vibration of the path you chose. If your path is the number 5, then the first year of your life was a 5 personal year. The second year of your life was a 6 personal year, and so on.

By adding up your day, month, and year of birth, you'll find your path number as well as the personal year that began your journey. You've repeated those nine-year cycles throughout your life.

Your current personal year is determined by the single-digit numbers of your birth month and birth date added to the current calendar year and reduced to a single digit (or a master number of 11, 22, or 33).

For example, someone with a birthday of September 15, 1951—during 2012—would be experiencing a 2 personal year.

Birth month: September=9
Birth date: 15=6 (1+5=6)
Current year: 2012=5= (2+0+1+2=5)
Add 9 (birth month)+6 (birth date)+5 (current year) to get
   personal year=2 (9+6+5=20=2+0=2)

A new personal year begins every January when the calendar year changes. However, the energy of the personal year peaks around your birthday. After that, you begin to feel the influence of the coming personal year that will begin in January.

Let's compute your personal year here:

Your birth month: _____

Your birth date: _____

Current Year: _____

Total: _____

Reduced to a single digit: _____

This is your personal year: _____

EXERCISE

After discovering the personal year you're in and how those energetic influences are affecting your life, what new insights did you gain about your career and love life?

_____

_____

_____

_____

Are you currently in a personal year when you should be focusing more on love or career or neither?

_____

_____

_____

_____

When you look back at your past nine-year cycles, is there a certain personal year when you usually fall in love—such as a 5 or 6
personal year? Have you found any patterns?

_____

_____

_____

_____

How might this knowledge influence your choices this year and
next year?

_____

_____

_____

_____

SATURN RETURNINGS

Your two most important life reinventions are around the ages of
twenty-nine and fifty-eight. When you calculate your nine-year

cycles and see where they overlap with the ages of twenty-nine and fifty-eight, you can see where these reinventions peak.

The first Saturn returning is designed to get you to reevaluate your life and the person you thought you would become while growing up. It's a time to step away from the expectations of your family and begin to see who you really are and what you came to do.

The second Saturn returning is designed to strip away careers and relationships that don't serve you and that keep you from being your authentic self in the world, using your gifts to do your true work.

EXERCISE

Are you in a Saturn-returning transformation right now? If so, what are you learning about yourself? If your Saturn returning was a while ago, reflect on what you learned about yourself and how that applies to your life today.

_____

_____

_____

_____

DAILY AFFIRMATION TO ATTRACT AND RECOGNIZE YOUR SOUL MATE

I wake every morning feeling deeply connected to my highest self and my sacred intuition. I realize that I'm a divine energy being with unlimited genius inside of me. I realize I'm here on purpose.

My true partner waits for me to remember this. The moment I remember who I am, my soul mate appears. The moment we meet, we recognize each other as gifted, intuitive geniuses with unlimited potential. As we open our hearts and love each other, we transform our lives and help raise the consciousness of the planet.

13

YOUR PERSONAL REINVENTION CHARTS

W HEN THE TIME IS right, it's right. So when is it right? Usually when you're in a 2, 11/2, 5, 6, or 33/6 year. Let's examine this . . .

PERSONAL-YEAR CYCLES AND RELATIONSHIPS

When you look back at your nine-year reinvention cycles, you'll notice patterns in past relationships that coincide with these nine-year cycles.

For example, most long-term relationships begin either in a 1, 2, or 11/2 personal year, when you're launching new partnerships; in a 5 personal year, when your attractiveness is in high gear; or in a 6 personal year, when commitment and family is your focus.

This pattern doesn't mean you won't date new people in other years. You will. But those relationships may be designed for your growth and to prepare you for true love in the future.

Your 6 personal year is a big year for love. You'll focus on your loved ones and give their needs priority. This year could bring marriage, children, divorce, or the death of a family member. Home and family will take priority.

When you're in a 9 personal year, every relationship will come up for review. You'll clearly see your partner's flaws and gifts and sometimes you'll feel like ending it. This powerful year gives you an opportunity to heal what's broken and bring your partner into the next cycle—or walk away. Friends and lovers from your past will also reenter your life. This is all part of the nine-year cleanup plan. You're getting a chance to decide who you'll bring into your next cycle and who you'll leave behind.

If a new romantic relationship begins in your 9 year, it will probably be a karmic soul agreement with many challenging lessons. It may not be the lasting love you're looking for.

On the following charts, make notes where you met new loves, began and lost relationships or jobs, and noticed big changes in your life. Review these life cycles and see if your previous patterns and nine-year reinventions can help you better understand what's going on in your life now and how to move forward.

BIRTH PATH CHART SYMBOLS

 Starting Over;
Reinvention Required.

 Begin or Heal a Relationship.

 Focus on Love and Family.

 Focus on Money and Career;
Finding Your Power.

 End a Relationship or Career;
Big Changes.

 FIRST SATURN RETURNING
Making peace with your childhood or leaving
it behind.

Reinventing career.

Seeing your path for what it is in this lifetime.

Traumatic event to help you see your mission.

Relationship loss or new beginning.

 SECOND SATURN RETURNING
Powerful reinvention point for new life and
career.

Stripping away of anything you've hidden
behind—leaving you to be your true self in
work and life.

Birth Path Chart

PY	AGE			PY	AGE			PY	AGE	
1	0 (Birth)			1	36	🕊		1	72	🕊
2	1 Year Old			2	37	♥		2	73	♥
3	2			3	38			3	74	
4	3			4	39			4	75	
5	4			5	40			5	76	
6	5			6	41	🏠		6	77	🏠
7	6			7	42			7	78	
8	7			8	43	$		8	79	$
9	8	♥		9	44	♥		9	80	♥
1	9	🕊		1	45	🕊		1	81	🕊
2	10	♥		2	46	♥		2	82	♥
3	11			3	47			3	83	
4	12			4	48			4	84	
5	13			5	49			5	85	
6	14	🏠		6	50	🏠		6	86	🏠
7	15			7	51			7	87	
8	16	$		8	52	$		8	88	$
9	17	♥		9	53	♥		9	89	♥
1	18	🕊		1	54	🕊		1	90	🕊
2	19	♥		2	55	♥		2	91	♥
3	20			3	56			3	92	
4	21			4	**57**	♄2		4	93	
5	22			5	58			5	94	
6	23	🏠		6	59	🏠		6	95	🏠
7	24			7	60			7	96	
8	25	$		8	61	$		8	97	$
9	26	♥		9	62	♥		9	98	♥
1	**27**	🕊		1	63	🕊				
2	28	♥ ♄1		2	64	♥				
3	29			3	65					
4	30			4	66					
5	31			5	67					
6	32	🏠		6	68	🏠				
7	33			7	69					
8	34	$		8	70	$				
9	35	♥		9	71	♥				

Birth Path Chart

2 Birth Path (Also 11 Path)

PY	AGE	
2	0 (Birth)	
3	1 Year Old	
4	2	
5	3	
6	4	
7	5	
8	6	
9	7	💔
1	8	🕊
2	9	❤
3	10	
4	11	
5	12	
6	13	🏠
7	14	
8	15	$
9	16	💔
1	17	🕊
2	18	❤
3	19	
4	20	
5	21	
6	22	🏠
7	23	
8	24	$
9	25	💔
1	26	🕊
2	**27**	❤ 🪐
3	28	
4	29	
5	30	
6	31	🏠
7	32	
8	33	$
9	34	💔

PY	AGE	
1	35	🕊
2	36	❤
3	37	
4	38	
5	39	
6	40	🏠
7	41	
8	42	$
9	43	💔
1	44	🕊
2	45	❤
3	46	
4	47	
5	48	
6	49	🏠
7	50	
8	51	$
9	52	💔
1	53	🕊
2	54	❤
3	55	
4	56	
5	**57**	🪐
6	58	🏠
7	59	
8	60	$
9	61	💔
1	62	🕊
2	63	❤
3	64	
4	65	
5	66	
6	67	🏠
7	68	
8	69	$
9	70	💔

PY	AGE	
1	71	🕊
2	72	❤
3	73	
4	74	
5	75	
6	76	🏠
7	77	
8	78	$
9	79	💔
1	80	🕊
2	81	❤
3	82	
4	83	
5	84	
6	85	🏠
7	86	
8	87	$
9	88	💔
1	89	🕊
2	90	❤
3	91	
4	92	
5	93	
6	94	🏠
7	95	
8	96	$
9	97	💔

Birth Path Chart

Birth Path

PY	AGE	
3	0 (Birth)	
4	1 Year Old	
5	2	
6	3	
7	4	
8	5	
9	6	💔
1	7	🕊
2	8	♥
3	9	
4	10	
5	11	
6	12	🏠
7	13	
8	14	$
9	15	💔
1	16	🕊
2	17	♥
3	18	
4	19	
5	20	
6	21	🏠
7	22	
8	23	$
9	24	💔
1	25	🕊
2	26	♥
3	27	🪐
4	28	
5	29	
6	30	🏠
7	31	
8	32	$
9	33	💔

PY	AGE	
1	34	🕊
2	35	♥
3	36	
4	37	
5	38	
6	39	🏠
7	40	
8	41	$
9	42	💔
1	43	🕊
2	44	♥
3	45	
4	46	
5	47	
6	48	🏠
7	49	
8	50	$
9	51	💔
1	52	🕊
2	53	♥
3	54	
4	55	
5	56	
6	57	🏠 🪐
7	58	
8	59	$
9	60	💔
1	61	🕊
2	62	♥
3	63	
4	64	
5	65	
6	66	🏠
7	67	
8	68	$
9	69	💔

PY	AGE	
1	70	🕊
2	71	♥
3	72	
4	73	
5	74	
6	75	🏠
7	76	
8	77	$
9	78	💔
1	79	🕊
2	80	♥
3	81	
4	82	
5	83	
6	84	🏠
7	85	
8	86	$
9	87	💔
1	88	🕊
2	89	♥
3	90	
4	91	
5	92	
6	93	🏠
7	94	
8	95	$
9	96	💔

Birth Path Chart

4 Birth Path (Also 22 Path)

PY	AGE		PY	AGE		PY	AGE	
4	0 (Birth)		1	33	🕊	1	69	🕊
5	1 Year Old		2	34	♥	2	70	♥
6	2		3	35		3	71	
7	3		4	36		4	72	
8	4		5	37		5	73	
9	5	♥	6	38	🏠	6	74	🏠
			7	39		7	75	
1	6	🕊	8	40	$	8	76	$
2	7	♥	9	41	♥	9	77	♥
3	8							
4	9		1	42	🕊	1	78	🕊
5	10		2	43	♥	2	79	♥
6	11	🏠	3	44		3	80	
7	12		4	45		4	81	
8	13	$	5	46		5	82	
9	14	♥	6	47	🏠	6	83	🏠
			7	48		7	84	
1	15	🕊	8	49	$	8	85	$
2	16	♥	9	50	♥	9	86	♥
3	17							
4	18		1	51	🕊	1	87	🕊
5	19		2	52	♥	2	88	♥
6	20	🏠	3	53		3	89	
7	21		4	54		4	90	
8	22	$	5	55		5	91	
9	23	♥	6	56	🏠	6	92	🏠
			7	**57**	🪐	7	93	
1	24	🕊	8	58	$	8	94	$
2	25	♥	9	59	♥	9	95	♥
3	26							
4	**27**	🪐	1	60	🕊			
5	28		2	61	♥			
6	29	🏠	3	62				
7	30		4	63				
8	31	$	5	64				
9	32	♥	6	65	🏠			
			7	66				
			8	67	$			
			9	68	♥			

Birth Path Chart

5 Birth Path

PY	AGE		PY	AGE		PY	AGE	
5	0 (Birth)		1	32	🕊	1	68	🕊
6	1 Year Old		2	33	♥	2	69	♥
7	2		3	34		3	70	
8	3		4	35		4	71	
9	4	♥	5	36		5	72	
			6	37	🏠	6	73	🏠
1	5	🕊	7	38		7	74	
2	6	♥	8	39	$	8	75	$
3	7		9	40	♥	9	76	♥
4	8							
5	9		1	41	🕊	1	77	🕊
6	10	🏠	2	42	♥	2	78	♥
7	11		3	43		3	79	
8	12	$	4	44		4	80	
9	13	♥	5	45		5	81	
			6	46	🏠	6	82	🏠
1	14	🕊	7	47		7	83	
2	15	♥	8	48	$	8	84	$
3	16		9	49	♥	9	85	♥
4	17							
5	18		1	50	🕊	1	86	🕊
6	19	🏠	2	51	♥	2	87	♥
7	20		3	52		3	88	
8	21	$	4	53		4	89	
9	22	♥	5	54		5	90	
			6	55	🏠	6	91	🏠
1	23	🕊	7	56		7	92	
2	24	♥	**8**	**57**	$ 🪐	8	93	$
3	25		9	58	♥	9	94	♥
4	26							
5	**27**	🪐	1	59	🕊			
6	28	🏠	2	60	♥			
7	29		3	61				
8	30	$	4	62				
9	31	♥	5	63				
			6	64	🏠			
			7	65				
			8	66	$			
			9	67	♥			

Birth Path Chart

6 Birth Path
(Also 33 Path)

PY	AGE	
6	0 (Birth)	
7	1 Year Old	
8	2	
9	3	⚡❤
1	4	🐦
2	5	❤
3	6	
4	7	
5	8	
6	9	🏠
7	10	
8	11	$
9	12	⚡❤
1	13	🐦
2	14	❤
3	15	
4	16	
5	17	
6	18	🏠
7	19	
8	20	$
9	21	⚡❤
1	22	🐦
2	23	❤
3	24	
4	25	
5	26	
6	27	🏠 🪐
7	28	
8	29	$
9	30	⚡❤

PY	AGE	
1	31	🐦
2	32	❤
3	33	
4	34	
5	35	
6	36	🏠
7	37	
8	38	$
9	39	⚡❤
1	40	🐦
2	41	❤
3	42	
4	43	
5	44	
6	45	🏠
7	46	
8	47	$
9	48	⚡❤
1	49	🐦
2	50	❤
3	51	
4	52	
5	53	
6	54	🏠
7	55	
8	56	$
9	57	⚡❤ 🪐
1	58	🐦
2	59	❤
3	60	
4	61	
5	62	
6	63	🏠
7	64	
8	65	$
9	66	⚡❤

PY	AGE	
1	67	🐦
2	68	❤
3	69	
4	70	
5	71	
6	72	🏠
7	73	
8	74	$
9	75	⚡❤
1	76	🐦
2	77	❤
3	78	
4	79	
5	80	
6	81	🏠
7	82	
8	83	$
9	84	⚡❤
1	85	🐦
2	86	❤
3	87	
4	88	
5	89	
6	90	🏠
7	91	
8	92	$
9	93	⚡❤

Birth Path Chart

7 Birth Path

PY	AGE	
7	0 (Birth)	
8	1 Year Old	
9	2	
1	3	🕊️
2	4	❤️
3	5	
4	6	
5	7	
6	8	🏠
7	9	
8	10	$
9	11	⚡❤️
1	12	🕊️
2	13	❤️
3	14	
4	15	
5	16	
6	17	🏠
7	18	
8	19	$
9	20	⚡❤️
1	21	🕊️
2	22	❤️
3	23	
4	24	
5	25	
6	26	🏠
7	**27**	🪐
8	28	$
9	29	⚡❤️

PY	AGE	
1	30	🕊️
2	31	❤️
3	32	
4	33	
5	34	
6	35	🏠
7	36	
8	37	$
9	38	⚡❤️
1	39	🕊️
2	40	❤️
3	41	
4	42	
5	43	
6	44	🏠
7	45	
8	46	$
9	47	⚡❤️
1	48	🕊️
2	49	❤️
3	50	
4	51	
5	52	
6	53	🏠
7	54	
8	55	$
9	56	⚡❤️
1	57	🕊️ 🪐
2	58	❤️
3	59	
4	60	
5	61	
6	62	🏠
7	63	
8	64	$
9	65	⚡❤️

PY	AGE	
1	66	🕊️
2	67	❤️
3	68	
4	69	
5	70	
6	71	🏠
7	72	
8	73	$
9	74	⚡❤️
1	75	🕊️
2	76	❤️
3	77	
4	78	
5	79	
6	80	🏠
7	81	
8	82	$
9	83	⚡❤️
1	84	🕊️
2	85	❤️
3	86	
4	87	
5	88	
6	89	🏠
7	90	
8	91	$
9	92	⚡❤️

Birth Path Chart

8 Birth Path

PY	AGE	
8	0 (Birth)	
9	1 Year Old	
1	2	🕊
2	3	♥
3	4	
4	5	
5	6	
6	7	🏠
7	8	
8	9	$
9	10	💔
1	11	🕊
2	12	♥
3	13	
4	14	
5	15	
6	16	🏠
7	17	
8	18	$
9	19	💔
1	20	🕊
2	21	♥
3	22	
4	23	
5	24	
6	25	🏠
7	26	
8	**27**	$ ♄
9	28	💔

PY	AGE	
1	29	🕊
2	30	♥
3	31	
4	32	
5	33	
6	34	🏠
7	35	
8	36	$
9	37	💔
1	38	🕊
2	39	♥
3	40	
4	41	
5	42	
6	43	🏠
7	44	
8	45	$
9	46	💔
1	47	🕊
2	48	♥
3	49	
4	50	
5	51	
6	52	🏠
7	53	
8	54	$
9	55	💔
1	56	🕊
2	**57**	♥ ♄
3	58	
4	59	
5	60	
6	61	🏠
7	62	
8	63	$
9	64	💔

PY	AGE	
1	65	🕊
2	66	♥
3	67	
4	68	
5	69	
6	70	🏠
7	71	
8	72	$
9	73	💔
1	74	🕊
2	75	♥
3	76	
4	77	
5	78	
6	79	🏠
7	80	
8	81	$
9	82	💔
1	83	🕊
2	84	♥
3	85	
4	86	
5	87	
6	88	🏠
7	89	
8	90	$
9	91	💔

Birth Path Chart

9 Birth Path

PY	AGE	
9	0 (Birth)	
1	1 Year Old	
2	2	♥
3	3	
4	4	
5	5	
6	6	🏠
7	7	
8	8	$
9	9	💔
1	10	🕊
2	11	♥
3	12	
4	13	
5	14	
6	15	🏠
7	16	
8	17	$
9	18	💔
1	19	🕊
2	20	♥
3	21	
4	22	
5	23	
6	24	🏠
7	25	
8	26	$
9	**27**	💔 🪐

PY	AGE	
1	28	🕊
2	29	♥
3	30	
4	31	
5	32	
6	33	🏠
7	34	
8	35	$
9	36	💔
1	37	🕊
2	38	♥
3	39	
4	40	
5	41	
6	42	🏠
7	43	
8	44	$
9	45	💔
1	46	🕊
2	47	♥
3	48	
4	49	
5	50	
6	51	🏠
7	52	
8	53	$
9	54	💔
1	55	🕊
2	56	♥
3	**57**	🪐
4	58	
5	59	
6	60	🏠
7	61	
8	62	$
9	63	💔

PY	AGE	
1	64	🕊
2	65	♥
3	66	
4	67	
5	68	
6	69	🏠
7	70	
8	71	$
9	72	💔
1	73	🕊
2	74	♥
3	75	
4	76	
5	77	
6	78	🏠
7	79	
8	80	$
9	81	💔
1	82	🕊
2	83	♥
3	84	
4	85	
5	86	
6	87	🏠
7	88	
8	89	$
9	90	💔

THE BEST LOVE OF YOUR LIFE

Welcome Home to Brilliant Love!

Congratulations! You've found your path and embraced your true work, intuition, and highest self. Your life is on purpose, and you're thriving in the flow of positive, loving energy.

Now your soul mate is standing at your side and supporting you in your great work. You've come home.

How do you navigate this relationship in a more positive and successful way than you have in the past? To ensure that this is the best love of your life, these 11 steps to brilliant love will help you fulfill your soul-mate agreement—the one you made before this lifetime began.

Once you and your partner are in alignment with your original agreement and you're both on path, love flows and grace prospers.

I've broken the process down into eleven sacred steps and explained how you and your partner can follow and practice them daily. This step-by-step method will guarantee a happy, successful partnership that nurtures both of you as you accomplish your great missions for this lifetime.

14

YOUR WORKBOOK FOR
LASTING LOVE

11 SACRED STEPS TO BRILLIANT LOVE

1. Understand
2. Give
3. Refocus
4. Laugh
5. Intuit
6. Forgive
7. Be Grateful
8. Sweeten Up!
9. Dance
10. Speak the Unspoken
11. Fantasize

Practice these eleven simple steps with your partner, and your relationship will live brilliantly ever after. Here's why:

LOVE IS ENERGY

Scientists and spiritual teachers alike have aligned themselves behind one idea—everything is energy. Everything you see, sit on, feel—the sun on your face, children's laughter, a good run, prayer, a great kiss—is all source energy. Everything and everyone comes from this raw material.

You're composed of this same energy—and its frequency can be raised or lowered according to your thoughts, feelings, and beliefs. The frequency you send out at any given time attracts like frequencies.

When we fall in love, our energy is at the high end of our continuum. We're pulsing with joy, passion, and confidence. We attract our partner with that high-end energy.

When the usual soul-mate complications, challenges, and karmas reveal themselves, we struggle to feel that original great connection. We often fall into blame and disappointment—which is our low-end negative energy. We struggle to understand why the fun, sweetness, and passion are gone. We slip into fear—forgetting that the energy we send to our partner circles through our partner and right back to us.

If you want passion and joy, you must become the source of passion and joy for your partner and for everyone in your life.

It's really all about you and your energy. Your relationship is a true reflection of the energy you're sending out. The quality of your own energy relates directly to your happiness. If you're embracing your path and doing your greatest work, you're tapped into daily fulfillment, inspiration, and joy. This good stuff energizes everything in your life. This high-frequency positive energy is where awesome love lives.

When you're lost in low-frequency negative energy, you feel unloved, angry, blameful, depressed, sad, guilty, and separate. Love doesn't exist there.

How do you improve your energy when your partner is in a negative energy space? Living on your true path and doing your great work is the first step. Reaching this level of positive energy creates an endless flow of happiness, inspiration, and joy in your daily life. You become an energy master. When you feel love and happiness—in spite of your partner—you rise to the high end of your energy continuum, where you have the power (energy) to improve your relationship. From there you can offer understanding, compassion, forgiveness, laughter, and sweetness—which all come circling back to you. When you're feeling fear, blame, and anger, you only attract rejection, coldness, and more fear.

The ultimate challenge in any relationship is to raise your energy to its highest frequency no matter what level of energy your partner is sending out. I have designed these eleven steps to help you do exactly that—raise your energy and help your partner do the same. At the end of this process, you'll both be basking in the love you've always wanted.

STEP ONE

UNDERSTAND

You have a soul agreement with your partner that you made long before this lifetime began. You've already spent many previous lifetimes playing various roles, including parent, child, sibling, friend, enemy, husband, and wife.

When you met and fell in love this time, you were setting your new agreement into motion. It went like this: "We agree that when one of us forgets who we really are and what we came to accomplish, the other person will remind us. We agree to help each other accomplish our greatest potential."

Think of it this way: you may be playing the role of mother, father, or breadwinner right now, but that's just a costume your soul is wearing for a few big scenes in this lifetime. Your higher self came here to use your gifts and talents to make the world a better place—to rise above "pitiful" thinking and fulfill a great mission.

Now it's your job to embrace your partner's greatness even when he can't see it and help him turn away from pitiful thinking—otherwise known as desperation and fear.

As you embrace the depth and breadth of your partner's soul journey and help her remember what she came here to do, you fulfill your agreement with her.

That's how you want to be supported as well. And it's the agreement that both of you made before this lifetime began.

Try this daily affirmation: *"I am helping my partner own up to his greatness and do what he came here to do. As I take that stance, he's better able to embrace my greatest potential. That's our agreement and as long as we fulfill it, our love thrives."*

To understand your partner fully, you have to know why she's here, what she came to accomplish, and what her gifts and challenges are.

The most powerful way to gain this knowledge is by understanding your partner's birth path (see Part Two). First, calculate his birth path and current personal year, then read the corresponding entries below to help you understand his journey.

Reminder: There are three methods of adding your partner's birth date to determine her birth path.

BIRTH DATE: MAY 1, 1960 = 22/4 PATH		
METHOD 1	**METHOD 2**	**METHOD 3**
5+1+1+9+6+0=22/4	5	May = 5
	1	1 = 1
	+1960	1960 = +7
	1966 = 22/4	Total = 13 = 4 (3+1=4)

UNDERSTANDING YOUR PARTNER'S BIRTH PATH
If Your Partner Is a 1 Path

Give her plenty of space and independence. Don't be controlling, or you'll bring out her worst traits of stubbornness and deep-rooted insecurity. Recognize that your partner's greatest challenge is to speak her truth, own up to her vision, and do it her way in spite of huge self-doubt. Once she does this, she'll become the princess of wisdom and strength—a leader and visionary capable of changing the world. This power is what you saw in her when you fell in love. Nurture that essence now rather than trying to destroy it because it threatens you. See her unique gifts and encourage them every day. Don't ask her to fit in to a conventional career. Urge her to follow her dreams as an entrepreneur, speaker, or teacher. Love her for who she is—a goddess. Don't be intimidated by her strength. If you empower her to follow her truth, she'll reward you with endless success, loyalty, and powerful love.

If Your Partner Is a 2 Path

You signed up to provide deep intimacy, communication, and nurturing, and to help him find a career that embraces his communication skills—as a teacher, therapist, or coach. Tread carefully with the words you say, or he'll be wounded and shut down. If he doubts your love, he'll get a little paranoid and defensive. Embrace his gifts of organization and detail work; your home will be orderly and clean. Show him you appreciate that gift, but help him see his greater gift of deep insight into others. Always tell the truth, and share your feelings honestly. Don't ever lie because he'll immediately sense the truth and lose trust. He needs a deep and honest connection with you. If you feed and nurture him with sensitivity and care, he'll bloom like a breathtaking orchid. You'll enjoy life and love with the most understanding, supportive, and sweet partner you could ask for.

If Your Partner Is an 11/2 Path

The physical beauty and artistic gifts of this partner will pull you into passionate love faster than you can blink an eye. But be aware that you're dancing with a high-frequency, gifted, intuitive, and spiritually evolved being. This is not a trophy wife to carry on your arm, no matter how beautiful she is. This partner will demand that you live up to your highest self. If you're not ready for that step, end it now. She's wiser and more intuitive than you could ever know. She feels every thought you think and can be easily wounded by them. This partner is an angel with an enormous mission to help the world heal. You'll probably join her in her great work someday. If you're ready to embrace your highest self and your true spirituality (and help her do the same), this partner will be the greatest love of your life.

If Your Partner Is a 3 Path

Encourage him to talk about ideas and embrace creativity in his work. Help him to move out of his head and into his heart and intuition. His comfort zone is living in the intellect and disconnecting from emotion. But he's capable of so much more. If your primary connection is through ideas and words rather than feelings, your relationship will be cold and empty after the initial sparks fly. He needs all-encompassing physical and emotional passion from you. He may be incapable of offering this himself, but if you can initiate it, your relationship will thrive. If not, he'll be the most interesting, brilliant, and aloof partner you'll ever have. Encourage him to create a business that embraces his creative and brilliant ideas. Working in a conventional workplace won't work for long. Yet he needs to make a living and not be dependent on others. Help him think outside the box and recognize that his unique blend of intellectual brilliance and powerful creativity can make a huge difference in the world.

If Your Partner Is a 4 Path

Help her out! Hire an assistant, housekeeper, and nanny to ease her if she's overwhelmed. It's also the only way you'll get to enjoy her company. Work will always come first for this one. She's up for any task and will give everything her best effort and then some. She truly doesn't understand how to do anything halfway. She's the strongest, most determined person you'll ever meet, so don't waste your time getting in her way. You'll just get knocked over. She'll need sweetness and nurturing to help her open up and remember that there are other things in life besides hard work. Encourage her to focus some of that enormous strength on physical activities such as exercise, hiking, and dance. She is already drawn to a healthy lifestyle, and making sure she follows one is essential to helping her achieve emotional balance and ease the stress. Her love of rules and convention may get exhausting unless you can help her remember the big picture. She needs a partner who shares the workload and cherishes her strength and worthy accomplishments.

If Your Partner Is a 22/4 Path

To keep up with this partner, you need an open mind and an inquisitive spirit willing to embrace new ideas and hard work. He'll be drawn to the boldest acts and most inspirational careers—especially the ones beyond conventional thought. If you're willing to embrace your highest self and spirituality and stand beside a great teacher, gifted intuitive, and someone whose work will long be remembered, this partner will be a powerful love. You'll probably end up working with him or you may never see him again. If you want a traditional breadwinning husband who comes home every evening for dinner, you need to find someone else. If you want to go on the most inspirational, and sometimes terrifying, journey of your life and feel that you're part of a huge venture to improve the world, you've found your mate.

If Your Partner Is a 5 Path

Get in good physical shape, stay healthy, and be willing to explore new worlds of physical and sexual passion. From food to wine to travel, this partner needs fearless adventure and frequent change. She'll never thrive in a conventional career, so don't waste your time encouraging that path. Instead, guide her to a career in the performing arts, natural foods, or alternative medicine. You may become obsessed with her beauty and charisma, but don't try to put her in a cage. She thrives on freedom and boldness, even when it sometimes feels wacky. She also needs deep compassionate understanding when her weaknesses reveal themselves. Keep the alcohol and drugs locked away (and sometimes the food, too). Open up to your own sensuality and be willing to share it often. Embrace her alternative ways of living and this partner will be the most fun and charismatic person you'll ever meet. Her light will light up every room she enters. Help her find her healing work and her spiritual center before she wanders too far off the edges of experiential, intuitive learning.

If Your Partner Is a 6 Path

If you don't want children or a deeply committed relationship, this partner could be tricky. He needs connections with many people, from extended family members to the global community, and he won't thrive in an isolated couple. Yet he'll want true love and commitment from you. A loving home will be a huge priority, and he'll long for children even when he denies it. He'll care deeply about all families—not just yours. And he may be eager to jump into local politics or community service work such as volunteering at the homeless shelter. Don't be surprised if he wants to run for political office. He has enough rock-star charisma to succeed. Loving and healing the world is his mission even though he sometimes criticizes more than instructs. It's your job to help him move from judge to healer. If he doesn't become a doctor, therapist, or politician, nudge his career in a more healing direction or he'll be unhappy and critical of loved ones, including you.

If Your Partner Is a 33/6 Path

Start meditating, praying, and deepening your spirituality now, so that when your partner reaches into the depths of the unknown, you can keep her tethered safely to this reality. She's able to see beyond the veil—which makes her clairvoyant and artistically gifted. Your job is to empower her to become the spiritual healer and teacher she came here to be and to discourage her from burying her sensitivities in drugs or alcohol. Music and theater are her natural gifts. She also needs classes in meditation, yoga, shamanic healing, Buddhism, Hinduism, Course in Miracles, energy work, and intuition, or she'll risk wandering into the dark side. Share in her divine discoveries as your own channel to the other realms. Encourage her to use the gift of channeling in her true work. Help her understand what she's experiencing and how she can embrace the sacred in everyday life. You'll never see such talent, charisma, and clairvoyance as in this partner. Be willing to explore unknown worlds and ideas without letting fear get in the way. If you're able to do this, you'll love the journey. The deep, compassionate, Christ-like heart of this beautiful soul is capable of transforming consciousness for all of us.

If Your Partner Is a 7 Path

Your job is to help your partner embrace his spiritual and intuitive gifts. This sensitive soul is hungry to understand sacred knowledge while still living in the physical world. His endless perfectionism needs to be focused on his highest self and the pursuit of the divine, or he'll drive both of you crazy. His creativity is a source of great comfort and inspiration and should be the focus of his career. He can become bitter, cynical, and depressed if he concentrates just on the physical world and its many flaws. He's desperate to know the higher purpose of human existence. He wants the truth, the whole truth, and nothing but the truth. His spiritual awakening must come from within his brilliant mind. He wants spiritual knowledge, but not dogma and tradition. He'll find his sweet spot where science and spirituality merge. Open your heart to help him open his to this multifaceted world. Teach him to meditate so he can tap into his right-brain creativity and intuition. If he gets cynical, pull out the quantum physics books to discuss the nature of reality. This approach will fascinate him, and you'll discover your best friend in these thought-provoking discussions. Take him to hear Deepak Chopra speak about metaphysical principles or Dean Radin discuss the science behind intuition. Feed him enlightened ideas and embrace his many gifts, and you'll have a brilliant, spiritual, intuitive, beautiful partner to share your life with.

If Your Partner Is an 8 Path

When you speak to her, stand tall with your shoulders back and your head held high. Hold on to your personal power. This partner instinctively looks for and takes advantages of others' weaknesses through brilliant discussion and manipulation. But this is not the behavior of her highest self. It's a sign that she's off path and not owning her power in the world. She must become a boss in her career, or her personal power will sabotage every job she takes. Giving away her power to others is not allowed on this journey, nor is hiding out and playing it small. She's obsessed with money, but that's the perfect attitude for her. She's here to be a millionaire in her own venture. It's your job to help her find confidence and jump into the workforce fearlessly—even though it may be the thing she's most afraid of. She needs to find the career that empowers her to empower others, and it must be her own idea. Enroll her in a business class, where she'll blossom with entrepreneurial ideas. Help her write business plans. Encourage her to just do it! She's abundantly brilliant, charismatic, and talented. Your job is to help her find the quickest path to financial success and respect. From there, she'll evolve into the generous, benevolently powerful being she came here to be. Once on path, this powerful spirit will be the wealthiest, most exciting, and influential person you've ever known.

If Your Partner Is a 9 Path

You'll be in awe of his powerful wisdom, charisma, and insight—as well as his physical beauty. He's capable of succeeding at everything he does—which makes it challenging to find his meaningful work. He's a wise and gifted old soul, and his life has already been harder than he'll ever tell you. He carries more pain in his heart than you can imagine. Help him turn away from drugs, alcohol, and cynicism that he'll use to numb the pain. Instead, guide him to spiritual awakening as the ultimate balm. When he's acting bitter and controlling, help him focus on what's possible in the future rather than what's gone wrong in the past. Help him see that his pain is meant to fuel his great work as a humanitarian or writer who inspires the lives of millions of people. He needs to know every day that his work has made a difference. Remind him that he's the teacher here and that it's his job to make things better instead of complaining about what's wrong. Spiritual focus is required for his happiness. His charming personality and boundless artistic gifts are his salvation. Encourage a career as a healer, writer, teacher, or owner of a nonprofit organization doing great humanitarian work.

UNDERSTANDING YOUR RELATIONSHIP NUMBER

As we discussed in chapter 10, when you add your birth path number to your partner's birth path number, you arrive at a number that reveals the challenges and gifts of your partnership. For example, I'm a 22/4 path and my husband is a 7 path. Our relationship number is an 11. This explains our intense intuitive connection, our shared desire to inspire and heal the world, and our deep sensitivity (which makes for easily hurt feelings). To truly understand the energy of your relationship, study the meaning of your relationship number and how it shows up in every area of your life together. Take note of when it enhances your love, understanding, and communication and when it hinders them. By understanding this in depth, you can create new patterns that heal both of you and that help your love flourish.

If Your Relationship Number Is 1

You need to make an effort to create vulnerability and intimacy between you. Practice the workbook steps 5 (Intuit) and 8 (Sweeten Up!) in this section. Schedule special intimacy dates like getting massages together and taking relationship communication workshops. Your independence is a given. It's your deep connection that needs to be renewed and strengthened. But once you do that, this relationship will be powerful and lasting.

If Your Relationship Number Is 2

You'll readily share deep intuition and intimacy. Yet you'll get your feelings hurt too easily and may bury yourselves in the mundane details of life to avoid relationship pain. Practice steps 4 (Laugh) and 6 (Forgive) in this section. Let laughter and forgiveness help you embrace the bigger picture of life and see how truly blessed this relationship is. With the abundant gratitude of step 7 (Be Grateful) and frequent forgiveness, you'll make a great team, whether you're creating a happy family or building a thriving business.

If Your Relationship Number Is 3

Having fun and being playful is easy. Your challenge is opening your hearts and quieting your brilliant minds enough to deeply connect and go beyond the words that come so easily to you. Practice steps 1

(Understand) and 2 (Give) to open your hearts. When you have that mastered, do daily meditations together to build your intuitive connection. Step 5 (Intuit) will help you with this.

If Your Relationship Number Is 4
Your relationship is strong, traditional, and enduring. You're both determined to make it work. But it will require effort from both of you. I suggest adding playfulness, laughter, and sweetness in large doses. You'll find those exercises in steps 4 (Laugh) and 8 (Sweeten Up!). But the most important work will be in your everyday communication skills. Step 10 (Speak the Unspoken) will help you.

If Your Relationship Number Is 5
Enjoy the physical passion and shared sensuality that this relationship brings out in both of you. Cook, travel, and play together as often as you can. This may be a wild and passionate ride, with plenty of drama, unless you center yourselves in daily meditation and honest communication. Keep drugs and alcohol out of this relationship, or things will spiral destructively out of control. You'll love practicing step 11 (Fantasize). But you really need to practice steps 1 (Understand) and 2 (Give) to bring depth to your partnership. Your hardest work will be speaking the truth to each other. Let step 10 (Speak the Unspoken) guide you through this process.

If Your Relationship Number Is 6
Count your blessings! This partnership is capable of true love and a beautiful, healing home. But you'll have your challenges, too. You may lose yourselves in each other and may never want to leave the house again if you aren't careful. And children will be a huge topic of discussion and debate. It's important that you build community together either in your circle of friends or with the family you create. This relationship won't thrive in isolation. Practice step 9 (Dance)

to help you each stay centered and keep the partnership balanced. And steps 4 (Laugh) and 7 (Be Grateful) will bring ease and grace into your daily lives.

If Your Relationship Number Is 7

You'll have an easy intuitive connection. And it's essential that you go on spiritual retreats and read spiritual books together, because finding divinity is one of the reasons you've hooked up. If not, your faultfinding tendencies could ruin the love between you. You need a higher perspective. Step 3 (Refocus) is essential for your success. Practice it every day. Add in steps 7 (Be Grateful) and 8 (Sweeten Up!) and you'll have the perfect lasting relationship.

If Your Relationship Number Is 8

Balancing the power will be an issue here. Who's in charge? You may end up running a hugely successful business together. Be sure you've written down who has the final say, or the power struggles will destroy your love. Your task is to bring fun and intimacy into this powerful union that has so much to accomplish in the world. Practice steps 4 (Laugh) and 8 (Sweeten Up!) to soften the energy between you. But daily forgiveness will be essential. Step 6 (Forgive) will help.

If Your Relationship Number Is 9

This may be the greatest love of your life but also the one you need to surrender—even though it may come back to you. This karmic relationship will teach you many important lessons, but it may be hard to make the union work on a daily basis. This major nudge from the universe will create great longing for each other and nearly impossible challenges beyond your control. To turn it into a daily lasting love, practice steps 1 (Understand) and 9 (Dance) to bring it into balance. Most important, practice step 10 (Speak the Unspoken) so that your truth is always brought to the surface. This could create the groundwork for your greatest love.

If Your Relationship Number Is 11

You've hit the jackpot with this deep connection, true intimacy, and great intuitive connection. You both need to get over your hurt feelings and enjoy this divine partnership that brings healing into your lives and work. You may end up sharing your great work. Practice step 2 (Give) to override the sensitivity. And use step 11 (Fantasize) to keep you focused on what you want. It's essential that you both practice step 7 (Be Grateful) every day and give thanks for this sacred bond.

If Your Relationship Number Is 22

This partnership will inspire you both with new ideas for the world and for your careers. You'll probably share your work. Your daily conversations will be inspiring and mind-altering. But you need to make this personal! Build intimacy and fun into your daily routine. Practice step 2 (Give) to soften things up around the house. And use step 4 (Laugh) to lighten the conversation. But most important, practice step 5 (Intuit) to build your intimacy and move beyond your great ideas into a deep, heartfelt connection.

If Your Relationship Number Is 33

Your otherworldly connection will be intuitive, creative, and deeply spiritual. The deep bond will be felt whether you're making love or cooking dinner. But you'll need grounding and daily practical kindnesses to make this last. Stay away from drugs and alcohol and instead pursue spirituality together. Practice step 2 (Give) to create a nurturing energy between you. And step 4 (Laugh) will help you navigate the mundane challenges of life. Deepen your already-profound intuitive connection with step 5 (Intuit) and this partnership will last forever.

IS IT TIME FOR YOUR PARTNER TO REINVENT?

In Part One, we looked at how our lives are bookmarked by the ups and downs, beginnings and endings of our nine-year reinvention cycles (as outlined by Pythagoras). Understanding your partner's current personal year is perhaps the most helpful knowledge you can garner from the numbers.

It's a true blessing to realize that his ups and downs have little to do with you and everything to do with his own path and reinvention cycles. You can support him so much better when you see that he is unhappy with his current job because he needs to let go of an old career and change directions toward his real life journey.

From studying his nine-year cycles, you'll be able to help him embrace change and move confidently into a new and better future. You'll be his greatest ally as he creates and experiences the excitement of his new adventure. And when it's time to let go, you'll be the voice of calm in the storm.

Reminder: here's how to calculate the personal year:

Birth date: September 15, 1951
Month: September=9
Date: 15=6
Current year: 2012=5
Total: 9+6+5=20=2
Personal year: 2

Now calculate your partner's personal year:

Birth month: _____

Birth date: _____

Current year: _____

Total: _____

Reduced to a single digit: _____

Partner's personal year: _____

If Your Partner Is in a 1 Personal Year

Help her start a new project, launch a different career, or go back to school. Encourage bold acts and big changes. Understand that she'll be busy getting projects going, with little energy left to spend on you. Being social or taking time to relax won't be high on her list of priorities. The weight of the future is on her shoulders, and it's best to leave her alone to get it done. She'll cycle back around to focus on you next year when her energy shifts and she's longing for deep intimacy and connection. You can support her best now by helping her let go of old relationships and projects from the past that might still be weighing her down.

If Your Partner Is in a 2 Personal Year

Plan a vacation or couples' retreat. He wants deep intimacy and meaningful conversation now. His new projects are moving along well, and he's ready to share the details. He doesn't want to work alone anymore. He could use your assistance getting organized. He's also extremely sensitive, and his heart is finally wide open. Be careful what you say and try to be supernurturing. Embrace this opportunity to deepen your relationship and heal wounds from the past. Share your dreams for a great future. This year could be your most loving one together.

If Your Partner Is in an 11 Personal Year

She will long not only for connection and intimacy with you but also for a deeper connection with God or divine source energy. She'll experience increased intuitive abilities and deep sensitivity that may sometimes be overwhelming. Share her passion for bringing new, uplifting ideas into your life. Join her on a spiritual pilgrimage. She'll search for inspiration in books, movies, and workshops and will hunger for the true meaning of spirituality. She'll want to discuss this topic at length with you. If you can open up to the conversation, this could be a profoundly loving and spiritually powerful year for the two of you. This won't be an average year. It's a year of blessings and deep healing for both of you—if you can embrace the new perspective.

If Your Partner Is in a 3 Personal Year

Have fun! Travel, network, and play. Join him in a new creative endeavor, whether it's cooking classes, dance, or home design. If you're feeling a need for quiet, send him to the party without you. This year he needs social connections to thrive. He'll have numerous ideas for a new business or book project; just say yes! Nurture those ideas and enjoy the fun of shared creation. Embrace his many new friends who arrive uninvited in your living room. His creative energy is a magnet for everyone he meets.

If Your Partner Is in a 4 Personal Year

Hire her an assistant, send her to the gym to exercise, and encourage weekly massages to help her relax. This year she'll have too many projects to juggle and feel overwhelmed with endless work, even though that work may not be paying the bills. Encourage her to get it done anyway. It's a nose-to-the-grindstone year, but the effort will pay off later. She's building the foundation for your shared, prosperous future. She won't feel very playful or social now—just exhausted and stressed. Schedule in some minivacations to ease her exhaustion. It's essential for her health and for the health of your relationship.

If Your Partner Is in a 22 Personal Year

Get ready for life-changing revelations and dramatic turns in his career. He may want to launch a TV show, write a book, or start a business that changes the way things are done. Just say, "How can I help?" He IS an inspired genius this year, capable of changing the world. But there will be lots of work involved. Be prepared to help out. Give up your vacation plans unless they'll be spent taking life-improvement workshops at Esalen or the Omega Institute. He'll be driven to achieve his greatest potential and unable to relax. Rock climbing or skydiving might be in order. Offer love and support and embrace this great new adventure.

If Your Partner Is in a 5 Personal Year

Join her at the spa for a rejuvenation weekend or plan your anniversary trip to Italy. It's time to share the fun, travel, and sensuality of this adventurous year. If she says it's time to move, call the real estate agent and make it happen. She's wide open to the flow of new possibility. Don't try to hold her back, or you'll damage the relationship. Set her free—she'll come back more loving than ever. Her charisma is at an all-time high, and she'll attract love interests and flirtations. Show her how passionately you love her, and things will go smoothly. Help her avoid past addictions by providing loving support. If your life is rich in shared sensuality and passion, she won't be enticed to stray. She needs stability from you now and a strong spiritual center to keep her focused on what's important.

If Your Partner Is in a 6 Personal Year

He wants true love and commitment above all else. It's time to nest, have babies, and nurture each other. He may face family drama from ailing parents or troubled siblings who need his help. Stand by his side and keep the fire burning in the hearth. This could be your most loving year as a family or couple. He'll want to focus on creating a harmonious home, but he'll also want to join community and political groups to make things better for the world. He may have health issues that need tending to. All of these factors will pull his focus away from career. It might be a great year for you to bring home the money.

If Your Partner Is in a 33 Personal Year

She's experiencing intuitive and mystical revelations like never before. She may want to study shamanism, join a monastery, or become an energy healer. She has a pure channel to the divine, so take notes. Her artistic gifts are heightened, and this could be the year she finally earns her Academy Award. Your job is to keep her connected to this world. Cook healthy meals, encourage exercise, and discourage any forays into drugs or alcohol—which could cause bipolar episodes and self-destructive behaviors. Join her on a meditation retreat and discuss Christ-consciousness, hands-on healing, channeling, clairvoyance, and other topics not normally on your agenda. Imagine yourself as an apostle standing alongside Christ to help him navigate the perils of his sacred journey.

If Your Partner Is in a 7 Personal Year
Give him lots of room for quiet contemplation and encourage him to write. It's time to explore the meaning of life and how to find spirituality outside a church. Create a sacred Zen-like workstation to encourage creative inspiration. Sign him up for intuition classes. Buy books on quantum physics and Buddhism and place them by the bedside. He won't be much fun at parties and will prefer to stay home and read. Inner reflection is required. His sensitivity is at a peak, and he won't enjoy working in a corporate office. This is the year for divinely inspired creations and new spiritual revelations.

If Your Partner Is in an 8 Personal Year
Money and career will be the topic of many discussions and arguments. If she's been struggling to find direction, debts will have to be paid this year. If she's been doing her true work already, this could be the most successful and powerful year of her career. She's required to own her power in the world now. Making a desperate career choice based on survival won't work. Nudge her gently into the world of big money and business. She needs to find her courage and take the stage. She'll thank you later. Enjoy your role as supportive partner watching from the wings as she finally garners well-deserved accolades and true financial abundance.

If Your Partner Is in a 9 Personal Year
Your job is to be supportive and kind and help him remember that it's time to reinvent. He'll experience career heartbreaks and relation-

ship disappointments. He won't be able to force things to happen. True surrender is required, a leap that could be very challenging. You can provide the spiritual and emotional solace to heal his wounds.

Whatever has held him back from his greatest work will be gone by the end of the year. These disappearing obstacles include outdated computers that mysteriously melt down, unhealthy business partnerships, and dysfunctional friendships. Be the voice of spiritual wisdom and remind him of his true gifts and highest self. Tell him what's possible in the future and that this is an opportunity for reinvention to a better life. If you've been unhappy in this relationship, this is the year you either file for divorce or heal and renew your vows.

EXERCISES

To deepen your understanding of your partner's path and cycles, complete the following exercises:

My partner is on a _____ path, and I can best help him live up to his great potential by

1. _____

2. _____

3. _____

I'm on a _____ path, and, to align my work with my path more powerfully, I need to

1. _____

2. _____

3. _____

My partner is in a _____ personal year, and I can best support him this year by

1. _____

2. _____

3. _____

I'm in a _____ personal year, and what I need most from my partner now is:

1. _____

2. _____

3. _____

Because I'm on a _____ path and my partner is on a _____ path, when we add our path numbers together we arrive at a _____. This number represents our relationship challenges and gifts. Taking that number into account, these are the ways our relationship works well together:

1. _____

2. _____

3. _____

And these are our challenges:

1. _____

2. _____

3. _____

Describe a grand and magical future vision of your partner living up to his greatest potential. Include the details of how he's making a living:

_____
_____
_____
_____

Now spend a few moments in silent meditation seeing your partner exactly as you describe him above.

Describe a grand and magical future vision of yourself living up to your greatest potential. Include the details of how you're making a living:

_____
_____
_____
_____

Now spend a few moments in silent meditation seeing yourself exactly as you describe above.

PRACTICE DAILY UNDERSTANDING

Rather than send negative thoughts his way, inspire your partner to think of new solutions. Here are three ideas to help you get started:

Share open-ended questions about dreams. Imagine you each have a $5 million gift from the universe but must use the money to launch your careers in new, meaningful directions. What would you each do?

Be clear on your own path and what you came here to do. Having a career that's in alignment with your own birth path may be the best way to help your partner. Become a model of someone doing his or her great work in the world—someone using innate talents to make the world a better place and to create abundance.

Practice daily meditation together as a way to quiet your minds and open to your highest inner guidance.

Take turns asking each other these questions:

How can you both use the information about your birth paths and personal years to understand and support each other better?

When you add your birth path numbers together and arrive at your relationship number, what insights does this give you to help you move forward?

Do you believe that your parents had a soul-mate agreement to inspire you to live a bigger life than they did and to help you fulfill your potential more powerfully than they did? Could they have chosen to do this by showing you who you didn't want to be? How might this be true? Discuss the idea.

Describe the happiest, most loving moment of your relationship. What were the elements of that experience that made it so wonderful? Write three things:

1. _____

2. _____

3. _____

How were you different then? How would you like to be today? Write your thoughts:

_____

_____

_____

_____

Write three steps you're willing to take to move in that direction:

1. _____

2. _____

3. _____

STEP TWO

GIVE

Your life will change dramatically the moment you realize that the love you've always wanted from a partner can only come from one source—God or divinity (whatever you prefer to call it). And only you hold the key to unlocking that divine love in your life.

Once you learn to open your heart, tap into unconditional love, and send it to everyone—regardless of how they're behaving or what they've done to you—your life becomes magical.

To receive love, you must become a channel of sacred love.

This ability to give love requires quieting your fear-based mind through prayer and meditation. Quieting the mind is necessary to opening the heart. Our monkey minds will give us a million reasons why our partner, child, friend, or coworker does not deserve unconditional love.

The fear-based mind eagerly points out our partner's many short-comings and mistakes. Yet this is only our fear talking. When we quiet the mind, we experience ourselves as pure channels of divine light, inspiration, forgiveness, and love.

A MEDITATION

Sit in silent meditation or prayer, using mantra to quiet your mind. After ten minutes or so, when your mind begins to settle down, hold your right hand in front of your chest, palm facing up.

Ask to become an open channel of divine love flowing from God to you, through you, and out into the world. See this divine love as golden light flowing through you and out of your heart chakra, right where you're holding your open palm.

Extend your hand out in front of you—moving the golden light from you to others.

Now specifically direct that love to your partner. Wrap him in the golden light. Hold him in that love for several seconds until you can imagine him smiling peacefully.

Get up and go about your day knowing that you've energetically helped transform your partner. You've given him a few moments to experience pure love. This will empower him to channel love back to you.

Now, let's put this love into action. Your first action step is to give!

Do something loving for your partner right now!

PRACTICE DAILY GIVING

Bring tea, make dinner, give flowers, put on favorite music, or take a walk together. This will improve the energy for both of you.

Write three actions that would make your partner happy:

1. _____

2. _____

3. _____

Do these today. Why? The energy between you needs to shift to a higher vibration before anything can get better or any problems get resolved.

Taking just one action to make your partner feel good raises both of you on your continuums. Only then can positive change occur.

Shift it higher by doing one loving action today.

ASK YOURSELF THESE QUESTIONS

In what areas of our life together could I offer more of myself to my partner?

What everyday, small kindnesses would my partner most like to receive from me?

What steps am I willing to take today to give more positive energy to my partner (realizing that when I take these steps, I raise the energy of our relationship to a level where love flows easily)?

Write those steps here:

1. _____

2. _____

3. _____

Remember: When we raise our energy (in spite of our partner), we connect with our divinity, which is the only place where true love exists. When we send that love out to EVERYONE in our lives exactly as we'd like to receive it, we no longer feel empty, lonely, or unloved. The unrestrained love that flows from us eventually flows right back to us—with abundance. Every drop of it gets recycled.

Here is the most powerful secret to having loving relationships: be the love you want to get!

STEP THREE

REFOCUS

What we focus on gets bigger because our thoughts give it energy.

When your partner is driving you crazy, it's because you're focusing on her negative traits, and the more we focus on them, the more energy we give them. Eventually we see only the negative side of the person we once cherished. Our energy sinks to the low end of our continuum, and the juice stops flowing between us.

When we're headed down the negative relationship spiral, it has very little to do with our partner's flaws and much more to do with our own negative focus. When we shift our focus to the traits we love (which is what we focused on when we fell in love), we instantly feel reconnected to our partner. This energetic shift helps our partner rise to be his best self. The spark is rekindled.

PRACTICE DAILY REFOCUSING
List qualities you love in your partner and why you love them:

1. _____

2. _____

3. _____

Read this list out loud. Keep it on your bathroom mirror and read it every day. By naming these good qualities, you're focusing on the brilliance in your partner. You're seeing his best self. This is exactly what you want him to focus on in you.

At least once a week, say to your partner, "These are the qualities I love in you . . ."

ASK YOURSELF THESE QUESTIONS

Has anyone in my life ever focused on my flaws rather than my gifts? Describe the situation:

_____
_____
_____
_____

How did that affect me?

_____
_____
_____
_____

Did their negative focus on my flaws help me love them more, or did it shut my heart down?

_____
_____

_____

_____

Do I most often focus on my partner's flaws or gifts? Give a
specific example:

_____

_____

_____

_____

How can I focus more on his gifts?

_____

_____

_____

What are three things I'm willing to do to change my
focus?

1. _____

2. _____

3. _____

Does my partner most often focus on my flaws or gifts?
Give a specific example:

_____

_____

_____

_____

Describe how you feel when this happens:

_____

_____

_____

_____

Share what you wrote with your partner.

TRY THIS DAILY REFOCUS
If my partner annoys me by _____ , I will focus on his positive qualities of _____ to switch my energy from anger to compassion and
love.

STEP FOUR

LAUGH

Humor is a wonderful way to tap in to our divine connection to
each other. When we laugh with big, openhearted, unrestrained
laughter, we recognize the absurdity of life and experience the joy
of positive energy flowing between us. It's a shared moment of
knowing that whatever problems we have, they are insignificant in
the big picture.

Remember when you first fell in love and laughter flowed easily? Probably everything made you laugh during that honeymoon

phase of your relationship. Do you remember noticing when the laughter diminished? Do you miss it?

Scientists agree that sharing laughter with a loved one binds us to them. It increases our happiness and ability to be intimate.

The many proven benefits of laughter include its ability to defuse conflict, reduce stress and anxiety, and strengthen relationships. Researchers at the University of Maryland Medical Center report that laughter boosts immunity; increases joy; improves oxygen flow to the brain; lowers blood pressure; reduces pain, fear, fatigue, and depression; relaxes muscles; and prevents heart disease.

Isn't this exactly what we want in our relationships? Less fear and more joy? And laughter is free and has no side effects!

At Loma Linda University, a seven-year, 54,000-person study found that people with a sense of humor have a 70 percent greater chance of surviving cancer. Researchers concluded that this was because of laughter's ability to increase human growth hormone (a natural immunity booster) by 87 percent.

Numerous studies have reported that laughter triggers the release of endorphins, our body's natural feel-good chemicals that promote an overall sense of well-being—another wonderful ingredient for a happy relationship.

According to researcher Steve Ayan writing in the *Scientific American Mind*, daily humor and playful interactions with your partner create a stronger positive bond and a healthy buffer against stress, disagreements, and disappointments. They also enhance creativity and problem solving—important considerations for helping your partner.

The neuroscientist Robert Provine, PhD, reporting in *Psychology Today*, found that laughter establishes and restores a positive emotional climate and a sense of deep connection between two people while diffusing anger and anxiety. He found that laughter is the fuel that moves relationships forward and that men are naturally drawn to women who laugh heartily in their presence. He also found that the frequency of a female partner's laughter was the critical indicator of a healthy relationship.

All of this research tells us what we already intuitively know: learn what makes your partner laugh and you've found the secret to happy and lasting love. Make your partner laugh every day and your love can overcome any challenge. The deeper your belly laughter, the happier your marriage.

During the most challenging events of my life, I've often experienced deep healing laughter that transformed the moment. When my husband Paul was dying, in the last moments of his consciousness, he asked me to do something for him that cracked us both up.

We began laughing huge belly laughs as tears streamed down our eyes. Our laughter filled the room with joy and spread to the nurses, doctors, and Paul's family members, who all joined in.

It was an exquisite moment and one of the few we shared in those painful final days. It pulled us out of fear to share a powerful loving connection that filled everyone with grace.

FROM SMILES TO BELLY LAUGHTER

This exercise will help you relax into laughter and raise the energy between you:

Begin by smiling at your partner. Smile at each other until someone begins giggling. Giggle together until someone begins laughing out loud.

Laugh out loud together until you're both roaring in deep belly laughter together.

Hold hands and continue this pattern for at least five minutes. No words. Just shared laughter.

If you're unable to share in this laughter release with your partner, consider the possibility that you need to become less controlling and release your grip on the details of life. The willingness to laugh requires us to risk some loss of control.

The inability to laugh freely with another is also a sign of spiritual crisis, a lack of trust in divine order. You must fix this problem; love won't thrive in your life until you address it.

Right now, remember a moment when you were laughing easily with your partner and feeling deeply connected through shared humor. Describe it here:

_____

_____

_____

_____

Tell your partner about this memory and what it meant to you.

PRACTICE DAILY LAUGHTER

Find a way to break the daily grind. Move out of your routine to find silliness and humor in life again. Plan three silly things to do together to rekindle playfulness.

Here are some suggestions to start the laughter:

Watch comedy movies or TV shows together until you're laughing out loud. It's a wonderful way to end your day.

Do something silly, like playing miniature golf.

Go out for ice cream cones.

Plan a laughter date. When was the last time you just hung out together and made each other laugh—without a chore to do or a problem to discuss?

Tell your partner about an embarrassing moment in your life and laugh out loud about it. This exercise will help your partner open up to shared laughter.

Look for the irony in your challenging moments. See the humor in your soul-mate agreement and how perfectly you mirror each other's flaws and gifts.

At the dinner table, ask your partner, kids, and friends to share the funniest thing that happened to them today, this week, or ever.

ASK YOURSELF THESE QUESTIONS

What am I afraid of losing control of?

_____

_____

_____

_____

Who am I afraid of losing control over?

_____

_____

_____

_____

Can I consider the possibility that divine order is always acting in my favor—even when I don't realize it at the time?

_____

_____

_____

_____

Can this realization help me feel more joyful and less controlling?

_____

_____

_____

_____

What would I have to heal inside of myself to laugh more
    freely?

_____

_____

_____

_____

Was I wounded as a child by being laughed at? If so, am I
    willing to consider that all laughter is not hurtful?

_____

_____

_____

_____

Am I willing to take one small step toward healing that part
    of myself to let love flow in my relationship?

_____

_____

_____

_____

How can I begin that process now? Write your thoughts:

_____

_____

STEP FIVE

INTUIT

When we define ourselves as different from our partners, we put them in a box. This blocks the intuitive connection that naturally flows between two people in a loving relationship. It prevents deep understanding.

The truth is that our differences are purely superficial. We may be wearing different costumes for this lifetime and playing completely different roles. But we're all made from the same—divine energy. And we're all on the same journey—evolving to our highest potential as we try to raise consciousness on planet Earth.

We've all been here many times before as men, women, heroes, villains, soldiers, and saints. We each experience every path from one to thirty-three (in random order) before our soul's evolution is complete. This lifetime, like all the others, is a limited-run engagement.

When we open our hearts and embrace this shared journey, intuition flows freely between us. When we close our hearts in fear and separation, our intuition shuts down—especially in intimate relationships.

When we fall in love, our hearts are wide open to each other. We're in the flow of divine intuition. It's nearly impossible to maintain this blissful, openhearted state 365 days a year. However, in our daily meditations we can open the heart and feel our partner's pain, challenges, and gifts. This practice builds deep connection and com-passion in our relationship.

If you want awesome love, stop seeing the other person as dif-ferent or separate from you. Stop putting him in a box. Instead, start FEELING your deep connection to him as an old friend on a shared journey of evolution.

Ask yourself if you have been categorizing your partner in any of these ways:

- You're a man (simple and unemotional), and I'm a woman (complicated and emotional).
- You're introverted, and I'm extroverted.
- You're rigid, and I'm flexible.
- You're emotional, and I'm logical.

Try saying these words instead and discuss how it feels to you: *"We're divine beings on a shared journey—each with gifts and talents we've brought to accomplish our great work. I'm here to help you live up to your greatest potential, as you do the same for me. This is our sacred agreement."*

Remember that we're all made of energy—pulsing waves of light. The goal is to raise our frequencies together and get on the same wavelength, one where love and intuition flow freely.

PRACTICE DAILY INTUITION

Write your thoughts on what it would be like to trade lifetimes with your partner.

Say to your partner: "I see your journey of pain, and I see your great gifts. I understand you more than you know. I will not sepa-rate myself from you, but rather take your hand and help you live up to your unrealized potential."

List the qualities that you and your partner share (such as a sense of humor, intelligence, compassion, love of nature, etc.):

Imagine you're connected to your partner through waves of pulsing light binding you together through numerous lifetimes in different roles. Draw a picture or write a paragraph describing this connection and discuss it with your partner.

MEDITATE TO ENHANCE THE INTUITIVE CONNECTION WITH YOUR PARTNER

Write your partner's name, birth date, and birth path on a sheet of paper. Put your hand on the information, close your eyes, and meditate. Quiet your mind with mantra or prayer.

After a few minutes, when your mind settles down, ask to see the mission your loved one came to experience. Ask to understand his pain and clearly see his gifts and talents. Ask what he came to accomplish. Ask for divine guidance to help your partner move forward to his highest potential.

Write down any guidance or images you receive—as long as it's wise, loving guidance from the highest source. (If anything ever feels frightening or negative, dismiss it immediately and repeat *Om Namah Shivaya* or the Lord's Prayer to protect yourself.)

Later, at a quiet time, share what you've written. Or use the information to help you understand and support your partner's journey.

PRACTICE INTUITIVE DECISION MAKING

To build your intuitive connection to each other, practice this exercise daily:

When you need to make a decision together—whether it's choosing a place to have dinner or deciding on a job offer—close your eyes and quiet your mind with mantra meditation.

Picture yourselves at the restaurant you're considering. Look at your surroundings. See and smell the food on your plates. Listen to the sounds. Now notice how your body feels. Does it feel good? Do you feel happy and excited? Are you smiling? If so, your intuition is saying yes to that choice.

Share your impressions with your partner. Are they the same as his? When your intuitive connection is strong, you'll arrive at the same conclusions time and time again. And when you follow through and make choices based on that gut feeling, your experience will be positive.

If your intuitive connection is not strong, it's time to meditate together daily. This is the greatest way to open your hearts and allow intuition to flow to one other.

ASK YOURSELF THESE QUESTIONS

Do I remember times from our past when we felt intuitively connected? Describe them here and how they felt:

_____

_____

_____

_____

How can I better open our intuitive connection now?

_____

_____

_____

_____

What steps am I willing to take to make that happen?

1. _____

2. _____

3. _____

What steps am I willing to take to change the negative energy patterns we've created in the past?

1. _____

2. _____

3. _____

STEP SIX

FORGIVE

Because you're a divine being who came here on a mission, it's time to recognize that you have been part of the dance that caused any painful or disappointing things your partner has done in the relationship.

Your powerful energy, past-lifetime karmas, and the agreement you two set in motion before this life began are all responsible for whatever conflict you're feeling today.

By recognizing that your agreement to wake each other up to your highest selves has been a catalyst for your partner's hurtful ac-

206 / SUE FREDERICK

tions, you can drop your wall of separateness and feel the connection once again.

Marianne Williamson, a New Thought minister and the author of numerous bestselling books including *A Return to Love,* calls forgiveness "selective remembering—a conscious decision to focus on love and let the rest go."

This can only be done when you recognize that whatever dance you're doing today with your partner is only a blink of the eye in your souls' shared journeys.

You've danced numerous lifetimes together and will do so again in the future. One painful step on the dance floor now is simply a reminder to clean up your technique, pick up your feet, and keep your eye on the prize—higher consciousness for both of you.

When we remember that we're all divine beings on a journey of evolution, great heart-opening forgiveness is possible for anyone. Whatever you say or do today is not the full story of who you are— it's only a tiny blip on the path of your higher education.

We'll all someday answer to our higher selves at the end of this lifetime. In that moment of clarity and soul review, we'll clearly understand every mistake and every great moment.

We'll recognize our fear-based actions and all the negative repercussions they caused. We'll understand fully our great potential and what we came to accomplish. We'll realize then that love was always the answer and fear was always the problem. As Williamson says, "Love is what we were born with. Fear is what we learned here."

Our daily judgment of others does not improve their behavior; it only weighs us down with negative, fear-based energy. Instead, our compassion for others, even those who wound us, frees us to experience divine consciousness and become our greatest selves, free from the heavy weight of anger, blame, and fear. "When people behave unlovingly, they have forgotten who they are," Williamson says.

In relationships, we agree to help our partners remember their divine origin and the great potential they came to share with the world. It's our job to remind our loved ones daily that they came here on purpose to rise above their challenges and to live up to their highest self.

A Course in Miracles, an alternative approach to Christian-based spirituality, teaches us that an individual's ability to forgive fully and without reservation is the key to that individual's personal salvation. According to these teachings, forgiveness is remembering that there is nothing "real" to forgive. Whatever we perceive that someone has done to us in this dense realm has had no real effect on our soul's eternal journey or our oneness with divinity. Forgiveness sees that there is no sin. Sin is the illusion of the limited perspective we experience in this physical reality.

As science and spirituality merge, researchers are investigating the physical and emotional benefits of forgiveness. Their conclusions mirror what spiritual teachers have long said: forgiveness benefits everyone but especially the one doing the forgiving.

Studies reported in journals, including the *Journal of Personality and Social Psychology* and the *Journal of Psychological Science,* found numerous psychological and emotional benefits to practicing forgiveness.

Researchers at the University of Wisconsin at Madison cite a longitudinal study showing that people who are less forgiving are generally more neurotic, angry, and hostile but that the more forgiving people are, the less likely they are to suffer from a wide range of illnesses, including heart disease and cancer. In fact, just thinking about forgiving an offender improves cardiovascular and nervous-system functions.

In addition to health, forgiveness has a positive impact on relationships. Forgiveness among couples produces empathy, compassion, increased happiness, decreased sadness, and a greater sense of control, according to the research. A report in the *Journal of Personality and Social Psychology* concludes that couples who easily forgive each other describe greater relationship satisfaction and greater commitment to the relationship. And researchers at Hope College in Michigan, reporting in the *Journal of Psychological Science,* reveal that forgiveness in relationships reduces depression and anxiety.

Other research shows that forgiveness can be taught and that when people learn how to forgive, they become less angry, feel less hurt and stressed, and become more optimistic, compassionate, energetic, and self-confident.

PRACTICE DAILY FORGIVENESS
Say the following to your partner:

I forgive you for _____, and I recognize that I have played a significant role in creating this transgression.

I have been part of this dance with you for many lifetimes and may have done this exact same act to you in previous incarnations.

I ask your forgiveness for those karmic acts we can't remember in this lifetime, which still subtly influence our current reality.

I understand that by carrying my blame, anger, and fear from lifetime to lifetime I continue the karmic dance that hurts both of us. I release it now for our highest good.

Say the following to each other:

From this moment on, past mistakes and painful moments are forgiven and forgotten, and we create anew the healthy, loving relationship we both want.

We no longer carry the story of our past mistakes because this story hurts both of us and prevents us from having the healthy life and love we want.

I recognize you as an old soul mate whom I've loved in many ways for many lifetimes. I'm deeply grateful to connect with you again now to serve our highest good and provide new opportunities for ultimate forgiveness and love.

ASK YOURSELF THESE QUESTIONS

What's one small step I can take today to shift my anger and initiate forgiveness?

_____

Can I bring tea, do the laundry, write a note, or touch my partner in a certain way to initiate forgiveness?

_____

Am I willing to meditate and see my partner happy and forgiving me?

_____

Am I willing to meditate and see myself happy and forgiving my partner?

_____

Am I ready to recognize that I am the source of all the love I want from my partner and that no one but me is ever to blame for my lack of love?

_____

Do it now!

STEP SEVEN

BE GRATEFUL

Gratitude is the most powerful energy shifter you can use in a relationship. This super-high-vibration feeling overrides anger, fear, and all negative emotions. You can use it to get out of any tight spot that you find your relationship in. (It's your get-out-of-jail-free card!) When you get gratitude pulsing through you, you'll feel opened up and connected to your highest self and your divine intuition.

Research shared in numerous scientific journals, including the *Journal of Gratitude and Justice, Journal of Personality and Social Psychology, Journal of Personal Relationships,* and *Journal of Social and Clinical Psychology,* has touted the many benefits of gratitude.

Like forgiveness, gratitude bestows health. Researchers reporting in the *American Journal of Cardiology* found that daily gratitude exercises such as writing about or discussing what you're grateful for created positive changes in cardiovascular and immune functions, including improved heart, pulse, and respiration rates. Another longitudinal gratitude study, conducted over a sixty-year span, found that people who are generally grateful tend to live longer lives and suffer from fewer diseases, including heart disease and cancer.

Gratitude also improves relationships. Researchers reporting in the journal *Personal Relationships* say that feelings of gratitude and generosity toward a loved one solidify that bond and benefit both the giver and receiver of gratitude. Everyday gratitude, expressed in acts as simple as picking up your partner's favorite coffee drink on the way home, strengthens our ties to each other. In turn, gratitude triggers a cascade of positive responses within the person who feels it that changes the way the person views the one they are grateful to, the researchers note. And Pepperdine University scientists conclude that you cannot be happy unless you can substitute bitterness and resentment with gratitude and acceptance.

Researchers at Southern Methodist University in Dallas, Texas, and the University of California at Davis conducted a gratitude study involving several hundred people and found that daily gratitude exercises created higher levels of enthusiasm, optimism, and energy while decreasing depression and stress. According to their findings, people who feel gratitude toward their partner also are more likely to feel loved by their partner. Gratitude encourages a positive cycle of reciprocal kindness among people as one act of gratitude spurs another—elevating, energizing, and inspiring its participants. End result: gratitude is interactive and enhances love and positive energy between people.

PRACTICE DAILY GRATITUDE

For a week, keep track of how many times in a day you express sincere gratitude to someone. Now double it. Make an effort to feel and express gratitude multiple times a day.

At the dinner table, share three things that happened that day for which you feel grateful. (Make one of them about your partner.)

Pay attention to the things you're angry or resentful about, such as an insensitive comment made by your partner or a friend. Now turn it around with gratitude.

Say, "I'm so grateful to be a source of abundant love and forgiveness. I'm so grateful to have one more day to fulfill my potential and make a difference on this planet with my positive loving energy."

Before going to bed each night, tell your partner and children one specific thing (such as how they helped in the kitchen or fed the dog or spoke lovingly to you) that you're grateful for. Describe the exact action they did and how it made you feel.

Before going to sleep, make a list of all the events and people you can feel grateful for. Send a "push" of gratitude to each person on your list—especially anyone you had a difficult exchange with that day.

Right now, think of two things about your partner for which you're extremely grateful. Here are some examples:

I'm grateful that you're a good parent to our child.
I'm grateful that you support me in my great work.
I'm grateful that you see who I truly am.
I'm grateful that I can talk to you.
I'm grateful that I can laugh with you.
I'm grateful for your wisdom.
I'm grateful for our passionate sexual connection.
Tell your partner the two things for which you're most grateful.
Ask your partner to tell you two things for which he or she is most grateful.

ASK YOURSELF THESE QUESTIONS

Can I remember times in my past when I didn't express my gratitude and regretted it later? Describe how it felt:

_____

_____

_____

_____

Can I fix that now by writing a letter or sending a prayer of gratitude that person's way? Begin the process here:

_____

_____

_____

_____

What is the benefit I receive when I feel grateful to another?

_____

_____

_____

_____

STEP EIGHT

SWEETEN UP!

We all came into this lifetime as innocent, pure, authentic sweet souls on a journey of evolution. As we've aged, we've learned to cover up our authentic sweetness in order to survive.

We've been told that we must be strong, beautiful, competent, successful, and wealthy to be loved. And so we've tried to be those things. Yet those layers have caused us more pain by separating us from others—and from our true selves.

Yet sweetness is our divine right—our authentic nature. It's a high-end, potent energy. When we show our true, sweet selves to our partners, they open up and show us their sweetness. It's like holding a baby. We see the sweetness and go there to join it.

See your partner as a baby smiling at you. Imagine cradling her in your arms. Speak to her using your genuine, sweet, vulnerable self and say

I see the sweetness in you and I love it.
I will bring my sweetness to resolve our challenges.
I will bring my sweetness to help us reconnect.

Extra Fuel: make love with sweetness, cherishing each inch of your partner and revealing your sweet, vulnerable self as honestly as you can.

PRACTICE DAILY SWEETNESS

List the sweet qualities you love in your partner and explain why you love them:

1. _____

2. _____

3. _____

Describe sweet moments you remember sharing with your partner and tell your partner how they made you feel:

1. _____

2. _____

3. _____

Write three ways you can share more sweetness with your partner in daily life:

1. _____

2. _____

3. _____

Describe a memory of someone being surprisingly sweet to
  you and how that affected you:

_____

_____

_____

_____

ASK YOURSELF THESE QUESTIONS

When do I last remember feeling authentically sweet toward someone?

How, why, and when have I buried my sweetness?

Am I willing to recover it?

What steps in that direction am I willing to take?

1. _____

2. _____

3. _____

4. _____

STEP NINE

DANCE

Every relationship is an energetic, intuitive dance between two
people. We fluidly move toward and away from each other. When
one partner leans away, he creates a space for the other person to
lean forward. When one person pushes too hard, she knocks her
partner off balance and throws the dance off center.

The silver cord that stretches between two people in a relation-ship needs a gentle tautness to keep the dance dynamic. Yet if the tension is too great, the cord will snap. If it's too loose, stagnation occurs and no energy flows.

How fluid and dynamic is the dance with your partner right now? Is one of you pulling away? Is one of you pushing too hard? Take turns describing how you see your relationship dance. Who is pushing? Who is holding back? Who is withdrawing? Who is ag-gressive? Describe how the balance of your relationship feels to you:

_____

_____

_____

_____

Now describe how you would like it to be:

_____

_____

_____

_____

What are you willing to do to make that happen?

_____

_____

_____

_____

Write three things you'll do to improve the dance:

1. _____

2. _____

3. _____

ASK YOURSELF THESE QUESTIONS

Can I remember a time when our dance was fluid and grace-
ful? Describe it:

_____
_____
_____
_____

How have I caused our dance to lose its balance, grace, and
beauty?

_____
_____
_____
_____

Do I remember a specific moment when I stepped out of
rhythm and damaged our flow? Describe it here:

_____
_____
_____
_____

What can I do to heal that now?

_____

_____

_____

_____

DAILY DANCING WITH YOUR PARTNER

Take a dance class together—anything from hip-hop to folk or ball-room dancing. The physical act of moving together will help you get more emotionally aligned.

Say the following to your partner:

If I've been withholding or pulling back, I promise to give more love and sweetness and bring us back into balance.

If I've been cold or distant, I promise to open my heart with gratitude and forgiveness and love you passionately.

If I've been aggressive and demanding, I promise to step back and hold you in loving acceptance and allow you to move toward me when you're ready.

STEP TEN

SPEAK THE UNSPOKEN

Every thought you think is written across the sky for everyone to see—especially your partner.

Whatever you're thinking and feeling is silently broadcast to your partner. When you have angry thoughts about your partner, she feels the anger and sends it back to you, creating a toxic relationship even when no words are spoken.

On the other hand, sending love and gratitude to your partner creates a loving relationship—even when no words are spoken.

If you doubt whether your thoughts and feelings can affect others, consider the work of the scientist Dean Radin, PhD, laboratory director and senior scientist at the Institute of Noetic Sciences.

"The bottom line is that physical reality is connected in ways we're just beginning to understand," he says. In his laboratory studies, published in scientific journals, Radin has found overwhelming evidence of our ability to hear each other's thoughts.

Your thoughts are tangible and measurable enough that they can be registered on another person's physiological responses—even when you haven't spoken them out loud, he concludes.

Radin, author of *Entangled Minds,* has spent decades in the lab exploring psychic phenomenon as evidence of our "entanglement," which is described in quantum physics. His research shows how our thoughts and feelings are accessible to everyone through the quantum field. For instance, two people separated in isolated, soundproof rooms can think a thought randomly about each other and have that thought instantly show up on the other person's physiological response measurements—such as heart rate and brain activity. When two people are on each other's mind, reports Radin, the "entangled minds model" can occur. "When I poke one, the other one flinches . . ."

What does this have to do with you and your partner? As divine energy beings made from pulsing waves of light, we feel our partner's feelings and hear his thoughts. Unspoken, these truths can create powerful negative-energy patterns between two people. When your partner is not giving voice to what you sense is going on inside of him, both of you begin to shut your communication down and begin to distrust one another.

Today there's probably an unspoken truth that's blocking your deep connection. It's stopping the intuitive flow between you and your partner. When we deny the truth, we make our partner doubt his intuition—which makes him doubt himself. This denial puts both partners into a negative-energy spiral. When we learn to speak the unspoken lovingly and with a focus on solutions, we break the destructive pattern.

Sit in quiet meditation beside your partner. Look into your heart and examine what you haven't been saying but have been thinking and feeling. Remember that our thoughts have energy and are felt in spite of the words we say. Turn to your partner and say the following:

> There's a truth I need to speak to be connected to you.
> Here's what I love about us . . .
> Here's what's not working for me . . .
> Here's a possible solution . . .

Be sure to include a possible solution.

Now sit and hold the energy of love around your partner while he or she absorbs what you've said. Then say, "Please describe your feelings around this so we can solve it."

Keep your discussions heading toward positive solutions.

Here are some examples of positive beginnings:

> I love our playfulness together and I cherish our loving family.
> Yet I need more time alone with you in order to connect deeply.
> Maybe we could leave the kids with my sister for the weekend and . . .

Your intention must be to empower your partner to solve the problem. In this way, you both ultimately get what you want. It's best to take turns doing this exercise, with one partner speaking for one minute while the other only listens. Then switch.

PRACTICE DAILY TRUTH SHARING

Once a week sit in mantra meditation quieting the mind. Reflect on what you haven't shared with your partner that could be damaging to your relationship. Reflect on how you might bring this to them in a healing way. Write your thoughts about it.

Go for a weekly Sunday walk or drive with your partner. First, share things you're grateful for about the past week. Then, share three things about your partner that you're especially grateful for this week. Follow that by saying, "Here's what I haven't told you . . ."

Share your unspoken truth in a loving way, offering three solutions to make this situation better for both of you.

ASK YOURSELF THIS QUESTION

When I examine what I haven't told my partner in order to protect him, do I recognize how this unspoken truth has damaged us anyway?

Write your thoughts about this:

_____

_____

_____

_____

STEP ELEVEN

FANTASIZE

Our thoughts and dreams have the power to create our reality. When we dream and imagine what we want to happen, we tap into source energy. We tap into the boundless realm of ever-changing possibilities—rather than our limited view.

By changing our negative beliefs about what is possible and instead seeing positive outcomes to our challenges, we set the energy in place to make what we want happen.

Usually we spend our time worrying rather than dreaming. Worry is a negative focus on what we don't want to happen. Yet the act of worry begins to bring that unwanted reality into our lives. We're using our thought energy to create what we don't want.

Let's turn this negative pattern around by dreaming of what we do want to happen. What would your relationship look and feel like if you were crazy in love right now? Imagine being divinely happy in this relationship one, ten, or twenty years from now. Can you see a shared future so wonderful that it makes you giggle?

It's important to hold these dreams in your heart as sure things—not as longing. They're simply going to happen.

PRACTICE DAILY FANTASIES

Draw a picture or clip a photo from a magazine that reminds you of you and your partner doing something happy together.

Draw or clip a picture of you in love. What do you look like? How are you acting? Start acting like that right now.

Draw a picture of you receiving abundant love. What does your face look like? Look in the mirror and re-create that face of someone who is well loved. This face is the one you want to show to the world and to your partner every day.

Imagine a future together that makes you giggle. Write down your "giggle dream" for this relationship:

_____

_____

_____

_____

Extra fuel: spend five minutes each day imagining a passionate, loving, and sweet sexual relationship with your partner.

Practice kissing every day: share fantasies every night for a week without making love. On the last night, pick your favorite one and enjoy it together.

ASK YOURSELF THESE QUESTIONS

What would your relationship look and feel like if you were crazy in love right now? Describe it:

_____

_____

_____

_____

Imagine being divinely happy in this relationship one, ten, or twenty years from now. Describe what it would look like:

_____

_____

_____

_____

Imagine yourself teaching others how to have loving, joyful relationships. What would you tell your students to do?

_____

_____

_____

_____

KEEP PRACTICING BRILLIANT LOVE

Now that you've practiced these 11 steps to brilliant love, you'll be-gin feeling a positive new energy in your relationship. Each time you hit a challenge point, review these steps, pick one, and do it with your partner. This method is truly the key to lasting sacred love.

Remember you signed up for this relationship. There are no ac-cidents, tragedies, or coincidences. You've danced with this partner numerous times in many lifetimes. Make this lifetime your best dance.

It serves your highest self to bring awesome love to your partner. At the end of your life, it will matter to you how well you loved people. And sending love and gratitude to anyone helps you fulfill your great mission here—to help raise the consciousness of the planet.

PART

4

STORIES TO INSPIRE YOU

My Intuitive Coaches Share Their Stories

FELICIA'S STORY

Although I'd never thought of myself as a woman who would get married early, I ended up marrying my professor right after I graduated from college, foregoing my lifelong dream of becoming a movie actress for the life of a faculty wife and mother. Years later I can easily see how my choices were fueled and shaped by fear—fear of my own power and independence, and of the possibility of real success.

As a child, I was witty, active, and smart. I also grew up with alcoholism, divorce, and other challenging circumstances. I got a college degree in theater and moved to California to start my career. But I quickly moved back to the Midwest when my former professor asked me to marry him. He was brilliant and old enough to be my father, and I was smitten.

We had children immediately. I immersed myself in being a mother, and as I see it now, was dead set on reconstructing my childhood by becoming the mother I wished I had experienced in my own life.

My husband convinced me that working outside the home was fruitless, and so I didn't pursue a career. I went back to graduate school and got my advanced degrees while raising my children. I worked as a teaching assistant for very little money, mostly assisting my husband.

After earning my PhD and going through a challenging time with my mother's death, I began to question my life, what I was (and wasn't) doing, and what I really wanted. I had virtually no clue about who I really was. I struggled to find a job as my marriage unraveled. I was depressed and desperate. Every time I got my annual Social Security report, I would weep. I felt worthless. I became obsessed with uncovering my passion and purpose.

I began a spiritual quest and read every book I could get a hold of on healing, intuition, and energy. I went to classes and became certified to practice a specific form of energy healing. I was pretty good at it. Yet it wasn't it. It may have been part of it, but it wasn't it. Meanwhile, my marriage was becoming more and more untenable.

After twenty years of marriage, I finally garnered the courage to leave. That was the most painful, difficult, heart-wrenching thing I have ever had to do. Before I left, I got my license to sell real estate and starting working. I didn't ask for child support or alimony. I felt I was jumping off a cliff—a big, adventurous, scary, exhilarating cliff.

Even though I was at an amazing turning point in my life, I still grappled with the nuts and bolts of redefining myself. I had worked diligently at developing my intuition, and yet it was not as clear or reliable as I desired. I have a practical side, and I leaned toward something systematic and less ethereal than just saying I was an intuitive.

When I studied energy healing, I trained in a modality that attracted me because it had a definable and repeatable system for achieving amazing results, even if you weren't superpsychic. The founder of that technique had been an engineer before turning to the healing arts. The big selling point of the method was that anyone could get healing results as long as they followed the instructions in the manual. I found great comfort in this. It worked. I didn't have to develop something entirely unique to me. I didn't have to reinvent the wheel. It was right there. Just follow the instructions.

But I continued to search for another way of helping people that had that same blend of practicality and spirituality. In the meantime, I allowed myself the freedom to actually explore my new world and enjoy myself in ways that were truly foreign and wonderful to me. While real estate was a fine jumping-off point to begin my foray into the real world, ultimately it didn't hold my interest for long. I continued to feel a pull toward a higher purpose, and yet, despite my intuitive skills, I still could not pin down my next career steps.

I was at the bookstore browsing the self-help bookshelf when my intuition nudged me to take the next step. A book with a white spine jumped out at me. I picked it up, gazed for a split second at the title, and brought it up to the cashier. The woman who was checking me out smiled and asked: "Oh, do you know Sue?" "Uh, who?" I replied. "The author of this book. She lives in Boulder, you know. I've heard her speak. She's wonderful." I looked at the author profile on the back cover of I See Your Dream Job. My college-age daughter was struggling with figuring out exactly what she wanted to do in college and, ultimately, with her life. I called and got her an appointment with Sue and also made an appointment for myself.

My session with Sue introduced intuition and numerology in a way that was intriguing in the same way that the energy-healing technique had been for me. It was a systematized technique that virtually anyone can master. And, for whatever reason, it's undeniably accurate.

Being introduced to my birth path number 3 and the personal-year cycles allowed me validation and a framework from which to launch myself into my true purpose. It gave me the fuel I needed. Even in my days of reading everything I could get my hands on about energy, healing, and intuition, I would never have picked up a book about numerology.

Yet when it was introduced to me in the way Sue introduced it through her book I See Your Dream Job and then through her individual counseling, it made complete sense. I found it to be a very down-to-earth approach to uncovering who you really are and what you came here to do.

I found that this resonated so much with me that I took her intuitive-coach training and incorporated key aspects of numerology into how I coach and teach clients now. Understanding my birth path has given me permission to commit fully to who I am. It takes the second-guessing out of the equation. Knowing this information encourages me to go with the flow rather than paddle upstream. As I become more confident in who I am (with the help of the numerological information), the more intuitive I become. One feeds the other. Today I trust my intuition in every decision I make, and I use it to help guide my clients every day.

As I embraced these aspects of my life, it allowed me to attract like-minded people who were also working on expanding their lives—including my life partner, whom I live with now. I could not be doing what I'm doing now without the amazing support from my partner (a 9 path), whom I met by following my intuition to go out with friends one night. My inner voice nudged me to speak to him even though he didn't look like my type. Within minutes of our first conversation, I recognized that he shared the same goals as I did: to live a life devoted to developing your greatest potential and using it to help others. When you're living openly and completely with this intention, you must be open to change and growth at all times. When you share this philosophy with a life partner, the intensity of fun, passion, and purpose knows no boundaries.

For me, finding Sue's simple yet effective way to frame who I am at my core and what my purpose is in this lifetime (through my birth path) has profoundly altered the way I see myself and others. It's given me a new career and new belief in myself—especially in my intuitive abilities. What a gift.

KEN'S STORY

I was born in Brooklyn, New York, the oldest of nine children, and raised in Massapequa, Long Island. My father always had a big executive job, so we lived comfortably, even if the sheer numbers of us meant that our friends probably had more toys than we did.

I went to Archbishop Molloy, an all-boys Catholic high school in Queens, New York. My high school experiences were the largest contributing factor in my leaving the Catholic Church behind, but clearly seeds were planted for my future as a spiritual counselor.

All of my teen years occurred in the 1960s, and I thoroughly embraced the sex and rock 'n' roll lifestyle. Those influences would define my life for the next two decades as alcoholism and drug addiction became my reality until I chose sobriety in 1988. After a year on probation and attending AA meetings it was clear to me that I was done with the substance-abuse phase of my life. I took those life experiences with me as my journey of self-discovery began.

I started studying metaphysics in 1994 and received my bachelor's degree from the University of Metaphysics. I became an ordained minister in what is now the International Metaphysical Ministry. In 1999, I was introduced to the works of Ernest Holmes and the philosophy of the science of mind and spirit. Eight years later, I became a licensed practitioner with the United Centers for Spiritual Living, the preeminent organization teaching that philosophy. I have been an entrepreneur ever since sobriety, specializing in coaching and spiritual counseling.

In 2009, I had the good fortune to interview Sue Frederick on my radio show. That interview, along with a subsequent counseling session, set the wheels in motion that changed everything about who I am and how I present to the universe. I have since become a certified career intuitive coach, but, more important, with Sue's help I have developed and now fully trust my own intuitive guidance.

Until I met Sue, I was pretty sure that intuition was a "woman thing," and I clearly was not a participant. With the intuitive insight I received from Sue's guidance, I have come to realize that we are all gifted with the same access to an intuitive self that most of us barely know. When I speak to groups, I remind everyone that if they think about it, they are familiar with that intuitive voice—it's the one they have spent their entire lives trying to outwit, outsmart, and override. Sue helped me to understand that I am not smarter than my intuition and that by ignoring it I was passing up the best guidance, direction, and focus I would ever encounter.

My metaphysical background has always had a foundation in meditation. In fact, I started meditation some fifteen years before I even became interested in a more spiritual path. Since Sue introduced me to my intuition, my meditations are definitely deeper and more meaningful, as the guidance I was once ignoring is now sending me into the world with a new clarity about who I am and what I came here to express.

Knowing my birth path and being able to tie up all of life's loose ends around my purpose has allowed me to refocus on what is truly important. And truthfully, the knowledge of the meaning of my 11 path has guided me to put my attention on what is important to me, but more than that, on what I am most passionate about. My life is full of teaching opportunities, from being an adviser every Sunday to the teens at Mile Hi Church in Denver to ever-increasing speaking engagements and interviewing all manner of New Thought musicians, teachers, and authors on my weekly Internet radio show What We're Thinking About. I also work with spiritual-counseling clients, and, as a result of my training with Sue, my career-intuitive-coaching clients.

There is another piece of the puzzle here that I do not want to overlook. That 1960s lifestyle contributed to a large extent to my always being in a relationship with someone to party with. This included an alcoholic and abusive marriage of almost twenty years that I finally summoned the courage to end after my sobriety made it unbearable.

Shortly before the divorce was final, I began a relationship that would last five years, but this, too, ended with that same unfulfilling feeling, but this time it was accompanied by pain. Because I was now well on my spiritual journey, a unique thing happened: I decided to explore how I might show up differently in a relationship. I embarked on a three-month journey of reading, journaling, and meditating on relationships. It was clear to me then that the key to a strong relationship was within my own heart. I felt ready to have a real relationship.

That was when I met my beloved Lisa. When I look back at meeting Lisa, I realize that there was a great deal of intuition involved. First, Lisa had spotted me in the church months before we met. As she tells the story, she had a little uh-oh moment, a feeling that I might be trouble. The day we actually met, we had a series of three brief encounters. We met in the lobby of our spiritual community, when I nearly ran her over. In a moment of amazing un-cleverness, I asked, "Don't I know you from somewhere?" Her rather wise-guy response was, "I don't know, Mile Hi Church?" And that was that.

We saw each other in the community center later on, and I asked her if she had figured out where we had met each other. She responded that it might have been another life. Again, that was that. But as Lisa was leaving the community center, there was definitely a small voice that said, Don't let her go. I chased after her and suggested a lunch. Lisa called the next day, and we set up a lunch date, preceded by four days of phone conversations. I didn't recognize it then, but those phone conversations allowed us both an opportunity to be our inner selves. We both intuitively knew what was coming before that very first date took place.

She and I have been in love from the moment we met. We were both following the same spiritual philosophy, and our relationship became anchored in a spiritual connection. The work I did with Sue influenced both Lisa and me when we each looked at our purpose and saw how we had been living on the edges of our missions. Now we had the information we needed to embrace and embody our purpose.

We had been trying for a good long while to find that one thing we could collaborate on as entrepreneurs. Once we both understood our individual purpose, we came to realize that the collaboration was not about doing the same thing, but rather about coordinating the efforts of our separate skills and gifts to complement each other. In the end, this realization has helped us to cocreate a life that reflects results that seem to be greater than the sum of the parts. The knowledge of our birth paths has helped us both allow our intuition to guide us and has enhanced our ability to focus on the direction. Lisa's brilliance organizes and supports all of my workshops, writing projects, webinars, and speaking gigs. I couldn't succeed a day without her at my side.

I can honestly say that if you follow the wisdom that Sue offers, the life you desire and so richly deserve will suddenly be a real possibility—not some faraway goal beyond your reach.

KIM'S STORY

am an 11/2 path Cancer. As I've learned, sensitivity and intuition are my greatest strengths and my greatest challenges.

Two years ago, I was off-path, off-track, and off-kilter. I was in a bad marriage, and I was depressed and angry. I had lost my career in publishing and was suffering. The only bright light in my life was my sweet two-year-old son.

During my six-year marriage, I went from being an optimist to a pessimist. When I tried to share me—the real sensitive, intuitive, spiritual me, I felt dismissed and ignored. My husband told me in words and in unspoken gestures that my belief in spirit, universal principles, shamanism, and intuitive gifts were all a bunch of hogwash. I was told I had to be conventional, and the saddest part is I listened. My sensitivity got the best of me.

I was as much a contributor to my downfall as my ex, and I know now that it was meant to be that way. The breakdown, rawness, and stripping away of the old me was part of my soul's plan to find the true me. My ex was a catalyst for me to step up and decide once and for all to claim my power and take control of my destiny.

As my relationship crumbled, so did my career. I was let go from my publishing job and couldn't find another one. Finally, one life ended and the next one began. The afternoon I left my husband, I felt for the first time in a very long time the return of the slightest, most infinitesimal sliver of joy. Each day since, I have felt my authentic self pulse stronger. Each day since, the joy of being me, of living the person I came here to be, of going after my dreams, of living my true passion and potential has blossomed.

Leaving my ex allowed me to see life again through a clear lens, allowed me to be open to my true gifts, and allowed me to see and seize opportunities divined by spirit. One of those opportunities was reconnecting with Sue. I had had a session with her in December 2008, where she shared my 11/2 birth path and my great mission. Unfortunately, I was still married and wasn't ready to hear her or take on my destiny. But her words entered my subconscious and began acting as flint lighting my internal fire to come home to self.

In June 2010, when I heard about her career-intuitive-coach training, I immediately signed up. In her class, I recognized one of my most profound talents—that I'm intuitive and can channel divine guidance for other people. I also realized how much I enjoyed it and that I'm good at it!

I would never have let myself own my intuition as a career had I not summoned the courage to leave my ex, close that dark door, and open the door marked, YOUR BRILLIANT LIFE AWAITS. I don't think I would have ever known what it feels like to be home.

It's been over a year now since I took Sue's intuitive-coach training and my life is blossoming beautifully! I'm doing the work I was meant to do, am emotionally and spiritually fulfilled, and am living an authentic life. I look forward to each and every day, and each and every new experience. I now define myself with my spirituality and intuition and no longer hide it or am ashamed of it. I've got a new book coming out called The Good Girl Addiction and I'm the cocreator of the SHINE Cards.

I haven't called in my soul mate yet, but I'm on the lookout. I haven't been ready, but I'm getting there. And I'm confident that I'll know him when I see him.

BETH'S STORY

On my twenty-fifth birthday, I interviewed for a retail-management position with a well-known natural-beauty-care company in Minneapolis. I was offered the position, and, with a little bit of hesitation, I left the department-store world that I had been working in for five years. During this time, I had a sinking feeling in my soul that my recent marriage was a huge mistake, but with my vows of "till death do us part," I had to figure out a way to make it work.

I found myself loving my new company and all it stood for. I was surrounded by amazing avant-garde people and a true blend of all races, religions, and lifestyles. I was finding my own identity and expertise as well.

I specifically recall one afternoon when the founder of the company stopped by and, after a bit of conversation, offered me a raise and a promotion on the spot! I called my husband and squealed into the phone that I'd been given a $12,000 raise and that I now made more money than he did. Little did I know what a turning point that would be for the two of us.

I grew with the company and was promoted many times. As a 22/4 path, I was more than willing to bury myself in work as long as I believed in what I was doing. And our natural-beauty-care products were making a difference both locally and globally.

As my career developed, I spent more and more time traveling internationally, which was incredible! My work kept me away from home, and the thrill of travel and meeting new people was wonderful. I was in my groove and was good at what I was doing. Everything seemed to be going so well—on the surface. And it did go well for a couple of years.

Then, suddenly, my body and all of my buried emotions spoke up, and I could no longer function as I had been. I was attending a global convention and literally couldn't get my head off the pillow. I was scheduled to do a presentation and spend the weekend with the affiliates who had traveled to the city for this event. But I couldn't get out of bed.

As time went on, I started to miss days and weeks of work, something I'd never done before in my ten years in the working world. Medical doctors told me I was exhausted, although the root cause seemed to be a mystery.

After a year of these health problems, my husband got a new job and we moved to the Pacific Northwest. The crack in the shell of our marriage broke wide open. I no longer had my identity and the lifestyle of my career. We were alone in a new, strange city spending lots of time together. Shortly after the move, my husband was laid off from his job. This was the start of big changes. The thought of staying in the current situation became scarier than the unknown.

The following year I moved back to Minneapolis by myself. The marriage ended, and I once again fell in love with my old career and the company that had offered me comfort, opportunity, and a sense of belonging. I'd been welcomed back with open arms, and after an awful divorce it was a soft place to land. I threw myself into work to forget about my personal life and also because it was all I knew to do—work like only a 4 path can work!

Then my body started nudging me again with numerous health problems. I ended up in the emergency room several times, and I faced possible colon surgery—which I declined in favor of taking better care of myself. I started eating better and my health improved, even though I stayed at my job. The following winter my bosses asked me to move to Washington, D.C., to lead a new project. My gut feeling was no, and I declined the offer twice. After the third request, I took on the project.

I'd finally met my match in terms of challenge and stress. Once again, I had severe abdominal pain and nausea that was off the charts. I rode the Metro to work and many times got off and waited at one of the stops because of nausea and pain. After finding myself in yet another doctor's office discussing surgery, the bell went off in my head. It was time to get off the gerbil wheel and truly make some life changes.

I finally followed my intuition. I resigned from my position and moved back to the Pacific Northwest to be surrounded by nature and to study energy work, coaching, nutrition, and the mind-body connection. I was my own first client and needed to get my body back to a healthy state before I could do anything else. I've since become a healing-arts practitioner and a career intuitive coach trained by Sue. I'm now enjoying optimal health and a joyful life and career.

I no longer hide from my personal life by losing myself in a job, but instead I am able to share my journey and wisdom with others. This feels like the comfort of my favorite sweater on a chilly day!

As a 22/4-path soul, work has always been an important part of my life. Over the past several years, I've found myself less interested in delivering someone else's message and more interested in sharing my own.

After taking Sue's training and learning about my 22/4-path energy, I now understand that I do have my own message to bring to the world. It has helped me comprehend my lifelong desire to help others and to make a difference. It has also helped me embrace my inner voice, or intuition. Following my intuition continues to move me forward on my journey as a healer and teacher.

I've learned to completely follow my heart—my intuition. This new approach (for me!) led me to meet my soul mate at a supper club several years ago, when he asked me to dance. From the first dance I could actually feel a pulling sensation in my heart. I'm not certain that I immediately recognized him as my soul mate because my connection with him is unlike any other connection I've ever experienced. Since that first night, I've thanked him many times for asking me to dance.

He's a Cancer 33 path and a very evolved old soul. He shares my spiritual journey and embraces my work as a healer and intuitive. My heart feels like it's dancing whenever I'm near him—even after seven years. I'm no longer pulled into relationships by the excitement of meeting someone who is the opposite of me. Instead, I spend my time with those on a similar journey. I also have a new and more positive-minded circle of friends.

In the past, I was so unsure about how to interpret my intuition. I'd blurt out, "I knew that," and people would respond, "Yeah, right." I started to be labeled as a know-it-all. So I just got quiet and stopped sharing things. When I became caught up in day-to-day details of my job, my intuition was really blocked. During yoga class, I would have lightbulb solutions to problems at work. But other than that I was pretty disconnected.

Now that I've learned to become quieter within, my intuition has become much stronger. As I've embraced this gift, I follow my intuition every day in absolutely every area of my life. When I feel the urge to go somewhere, call someone, or do something, I follow it! I now realize that everything is in divine order, and, when I live intuitively, things turn out better than I could have planned.

CHI CHI'S STORY

On February 19, 1999, I was working as a contract administrator for the Department of Energy and also doing nonprofit-development coaching. Everything was hunky-dory. I was in the career of my choice, helping others develop successful nonprofit organizations, and happy as a wife and mother. At this time, I had an MBA and a BA in public relations. I had everything: the house with the white picket fence, the dog, the cars, the family, and money to shop 'til I dropped. I understand now that I'm a birth path 9 and came here to rise to my highest self. Life was about to teach me how to do that.

February 19 is my birthday, and it was also the day that I worked long and hard to complete a grant for one of my clients. My husband dropped in to wish me a happy birthday and then left to prepare my surprise birthday party. I hastily kissed him good-bye so I could continue with my work. I never saw him again.

I spent most of the evening working in my office to finish the grant because I had to mail it out that night. I finally completed it and had a friend drop me off at my house. Upon my arrival, I noticed that a strong cloud of gloom manifested inside of me. At first, I thought I was tired from all the work I had done that day. Instead, the life I took for granted and the husband I loved were gone in a matter of seconds. I was greeted by the Knoxville Police Department and asked to identify the body of my husband. He had been in a car accident.

My transition to the life I have now did not take place immediately. But when it did, I was able to realize my true calling. From a series of other losses that same year, including losing my job, I was left with the greatest gift of all, a relationship with God. After a period of grieving, I accepted my mission to serve as a spiritual life coach, providing tools to help others align with their inner purpose.

My life is very different now. My misery became my ministry. I have since found my soul mate—a 6-path soul whom I recognized instantly. My current husband brings me balance, joy, and restoration of all that I thought I had lost. Today I realize that the life I lived was an illusion. The love for my husband was real, but the work I was doing was not my true path. I came to realize that my true path was giving to others everything I wanted for myself: alignment, balance, and the feeling of being whole again.

Life is not a box of chocolates but a journey of challenges and choices that help you develop into your true self. I realize that now, and I help others embrace it. I've taken Sue's intuitive-coach training and spend my time guiding others using intuition and the birth path information.

Understanding my birth path has clarified my own life mission. My personal-year cycle has pinpointed the challenges I designed for this lifetime. Trusting my intuition has strengthened my relationship with God and helped me develop more confidence in my work. Intuition allows me to solely depend on what the universe brings to me for my clients instead of listening to ego—which can be destructive. I'm grateful to be where I am today.

GARY'S STORY

'm a Taurus 5 birth path. As a Taurus, I'm drawn to the practical and to being grounded. It was easy to apply these tendencies to practical-work issues and build a career around them. I created better processes, procedures, and systems in the workplace. And I was good at it. But as a 5 path, I came to see myself more as an explorer or a pathfinder leading people to a better life. While I had glimpses of this insight, it wasn't until I truly understood what a Taurus on a 5 path was all about that I began to embrace this aspect of myself. This realization meant I had to change careers even though change is frightening to me.

Working with Sue, the pieces of the puzzle started to fall into place. The conflicts in my thinking, my dreams, what I was good at all of a sudden made sense. And these random, distinct aspects of my life no longer left me confused. Instead, a mosaic of who I am finally emerged.

Once I understood this I began to better understand who I am, which led to acceptance. I am a strategic planner, among many other things—and it was like getting this personal strategic plan. "Oh! OK so this is what it's all about. I can work with this, and, wow, it makes sense and makes me feel pretty good about myself," I realized.

Over the years, I had come to believe in intuition but never really trusted it. I always overanalyzed everything, feeling I had to make the perfect decision every time and I could not trust gut decisions. As I achieved success in my professional life and found myself leading and teaching people, I felt a sense of security that allowed me to act more impulsively. Often those impulsive actions were brilliant. I often thought, Where did that come from? But I knew I liked it and began to honor it.

This trust bled over big-time into my love life when I met my wife and proposed to her. I had made some bad choices in relationships in my life. While I was hoping to find a life partner, I was playing it safe in dating. I first met Elizabeth (a 1 path) through a group of friends, and for both of us there wasn't an initial attraction. We got to know one another slowly, and I came to gain a respect and admiration for her strength and depth of character. A casual dinner ignited our interest in one another, and we began seeing each other in a very different light.

We started dating but immediately we knew we were in a serious relationship. After a couple of dates we were having a magical day together in New York City, where we both live, and this absurd thought kept coming into my mind, Ask her to marry you! I kept dismissing that thought, judging it as impulsive and way too soon.

Later that day, we were talking about a three-thousand-year-old wooden Buddha relief we admired at an art fair earlier in the day, and Elizabeth revealed that she had thought about asking me to marry her while we stood admiring it (exactly when I had had the same thought). When she said that, I was flooded with the thoughts that came to me throughout the day, and it was a moment when time stood still for me. I knew what I wanted, what the universe was offering to me in that moment, and I knew I could dismiss it and play it safe. But I also knew my truth. I followed my intuition and asked her to marry me right then. Thank God, she accepted. Would she have accepted if I had waited months or a year? Probably, but honoring my truth, listening to that voice within me, was me showing up in my life and accepting the moment. And accepting my intuition! It was one of the finer moments in my life.

Meanwhile, I knew that I wanted to help others through my work using my wisdom and insight, gained through the pain of my lifetime journey. I had struggled with addictions and had become sober years ago. I already knew I could help others who struggled with addiction. This resonated with me, but again the practical Taurus was saying that I needed the safety of a corporate job. While I had experienced tremendous growth in the corporate world, it was feeling more restricting and less challenging. During a session with Sue, when she had presented me a vision of the future, where I was profoundly helping people in finding their own strength and path, I did indeed giggle from happiness. Eventually I began to take baby steps inspired by that vision. One step was becoming certified as a professional life coach. As I started working with clients, I found that, by quieting my mind and listening to the client, I would have insights about the client that I could share. It usually started with, "This is what is coming up for me . . ." And those insights had a profound impact on the client, which of course gave me the confidence to listen more and not judge my inner voice. I was learning to own my intuition. Yet I still juggled my corporate job with my life-coaching practice—afraid to let the corporate gig go.

During another crisis in my corporate career, I decided to take Sue's intuitive-coaching course. I had never considered doing it because I did not view myself as intuitive. Yeah, I had heard that we all have intuitive abilities, and in fact I was relying on intuition in my life-coaching practice. But I didn't believe I was capable of sitting and meditating to intentionally receive guidance intuitively.

But I was vulnerable in that corporate career crisis. So I took the weekend course. It wasn't the first time I found myself the only guy in a group of female advanced souls. Nevertheless, it was intimidating until we started getting into the course work and exercises. I resonated with Sue's approach to using numerology and intuition to help find your mission in this lifetime. I had already done some numerology readings with friends based on the book I See Your Dream Job, but the coaching course took it to a whole other level. And the pieces of the puzzle fell into place. This system works and makes sense, and I found that coaching using this system was very powerful. I also learned that I'm very good at it. This turned out be helpful when I was eventually let go from the corporate job I was unhappy with. Now I'm making my living entirely through my coaching and consulting.

During my sessions with clients, I keep open to my intuitive thoughts, and I trust that my intuition will come through during the session. This has resulted in my being more open and trusting of my intuition in general in my life. By the way, when I hear a client tell me that our session was amazing and profound, I get this warm feeling inside and I giggle to myself.

WENDY'S STORY

Listening to one's intuition. It's an idea that seems easy to understand intellectually. Listen to your gut, they say. What does your gut tell you? What is a gut? When I "feel" something, when I experience the "truth" or the "beauty" of something, when I look at a Rothko painting, for example, I feel the overwhelming emotional power of that painting in my chest. The pressure of something so deep and true is in my chest. Is that where my intuition is speaking to me?

It took me years to learn how to separate my head from my heart—my thinking from my feeling. Perhaps if I had met Sue Frederick years ago, I could have made the leap then toward recognizing the role meditation plays in revealing this "listening" place inside myself. I would have had the tools to interpret the signs and messages and distinguish hurtful from helpful. I would have acted as a warrior to claim my spiritual birthright each time I chose joy and creative expression—rather than dependency and need.

I tried to make sense of things from what I thought to be a karmic point of view. But I did not fully know how to navigate the pitfalls of that karma before meeting Sue, whose mission is to have all souls recognize what their greater purpose in this life is. Her notion that I signed up for this life and that my mission involves affecting change in other people's lives has woken up my sense of responsibility. It has allowed me to step up my game.

Learning that an individual's birth path number is influenced by his or her zodiac sign and impacted by the current year in a progressive nine-year cycle was like discovering the existence of the earth's harmonic convergence. It's an invisible code, a skeletal structure that anchors and helps us interpret our human experience.

Knowing that I'm in my 9 personal year helps to explain the dismantling experiences of that year. Knowing that I'm in my 1 personal year explains that I am at the germinating stage of a new idea, not riding its zenith. Inherent in this self-interpretation is the self-grace that would otherwise be elusive. I give myself permission to be in breakdown in my ninth personal year. I forgive myself that success has eluded me in my 1 personal year.

Saturn's return is another piece of the puzzle with resonating power that Sue has recognized. Without a prior working knowledge of astrology, I can now understand the planet Saturn's role in each and every one of our mapped personal trajectories.

With these four elements in place, our "intuition" and life experiences flood in to connect the dots. Life makes sense. Our mission becomes clear.

In her private sessions, workshops, and books, Sue brings to consciousness this vital and dynamic life lesson: if you're not experiencing joy and self-expression in your work and in your love relationship, you are not on your life path. You are not living the expression of your life's purpose. And living our life's purpose is what we are put on earth to do. It is our personal mission to find it, live it, and, most important, share it with the world.

Live on the light side of your birth path number. Climb out of the dark side by choosing to be true to your birth path's grace and strength. And in claiming your spiritual birthright, transform others' lives with your realizations, stories, and life journey. This is what I've learned from Sue.

BIBLIOGRAPHY

Algoe, Sara B., Gable, Shelly L., Maisel, Natalya C. (2012). "It's The Little Things: Everyday Gratitude as a Booster Shot for Romantic Relationships." *Personal Relationships* D01: 10: 1111KJ. 1475–6811.

Atmanspacher, H., Romer, H., and Walach H. (2002). "Weak Quantum Theory: Complementing and Entanglement in Physics and Beyond." *Foundations of Physics* 32 (3), 379–406.

Berk, Lee S., MPH, MD, PhD, Felten, David L., MD, PhD, Tan, Stanley A., MD, PhD, Bittman, Barry B., MD, and Westengard, James, BS. (2001). "Modulation of Neuroimmune Parameters During the Eustress of Humor-Associated Mirthful Laughter Alternative Therapies." Vol. 7, No. 2.

Berry, J. W., Worthington, E. L., Parrot, I. L., O'Connor, L. E., & Wade, N.G. (2001). "Dispositional Forgiveness: Development and Construct Validity of the Transgression Narrative Test of Forgiveness (TNTF)." *Personality & Social Psychology Bulletin*, 1277–1290.

Emmons, R. A., and McCullough, M. E. (2003). "Counting Blessings Versus Burdens: Experimental Studies of Gratitude and Subjective Well-Being in Daily Life." *Journal of Personality and Social Psychology* 84: 377–389.

Graves, Robert. *Poetic Craft and Principle* (London: Cassell, 1976), p. 138.

Kerns, Charles D., PhD (2006). "Counting Your Blessings Will Benefit Yourself and Your Organization." *Graziado Business Review*. Pepperdine University. Volume 9, Issue 4.

Lutz, A, et al. (2004). "Long-Term Meditators Self-Induce High-Amplitude Gamma Synchrony During Mental Practice." *Proceedings of the National Academy of Science* 101 (46) 19369–73.

McCraty, R., Atkinson, M., Tiller, W., Rein, G., and Watkins, A. D. (1995). "The Effects of Emotions on Short-Term Power Spectrum Analysis of Heart Rate Variability" *American Journal of Cardiology* 76: 1089–1093

McCullough, M. E., Worthington, E. L., Jr., and Rachel, K. C. (1997). "Interpersonal Forgiving in Close Relationships." *Journal of Personality and Social Psychology* 73, 321–336.

Miller, Michael, MD, Clark, Adam, MD, Seidler, Alexander, PhD "Laughter Is the Best Medicine for Your Heart." Proceedings of Presented Papers: The 73rd Scientific Session of the American Heart Association. New Orleans, Louisiana: November 15, 2000.

Paul-Labrador, Maura, et al. (2006) "Meditation May Improve Cardiac Risk Factors in Patients with Coronary Heart Disease." *Archives of Internal Medicine* 166: 1218–1224.

Provine, Robert, PhD. *Laughter: A Scientific Investigation*. (New York: Penguin Books, 2001).

Radin, D. I. (2005). "The Sense of Being Stared At." *Journal of Consciousness Studies* 12 (6): (95–100).

Radin, Dean, PhD. *The Conscious Universe*. (New York: Harper One, 1997).

———.*Entangled Minds*. (New York: Paraview, 2006).

Taylor, Jill Bolte. *My Stroke of Insight*. (New York: Viking Press, 2006).

Williamson, Marianne. *A Return to Love: Reflections on the Principles of a Course in Miracles*. (New York: HarperCollins Publishers, 1992).

Witvliet, C.V.O., Ludwig, T. E., & Vander Laan, K. L. (2001). "Granting Forgiveness of Harboring Grudges: Implications for Emotion, Physiology, and Health." *Journal of Psychological Science* 12, 117–123.

ABOUT THE AUTHOR

Intuitive Sue Frederick's work, described as "a breath of fresh air" and "an enlightened new perspective," has been featured in *The New York Times*, *Real Simple*, *Complete Woman*, *Yoga Journal*, *Fit Yoga*, and *Woman's World* and on CNN.com. She's been a guest on more than two hundred radio shows and numerous TV shows, including *Bridging Heaven and Earth*. Her workshop venues include the New York Learning Annex; Omega Institute in Rhinebeck, New York; Naropa University; Loyola University; National Hospice Association; the American Business Women's Association; and the National Career Development Association. As an intuitive since childhood, Sue draws on dreams, numerology, and conversations with spirits to help you "see your soul mate." She's the author of *I See Your Dream Job: A Career Intuitive Shows You How to Discover What You Were Put on Earth to Do* (St. Martin's Press) and *Dancing at Your Desk: A Metaphysical Guide to Job Happiness*. To learn more about her work and to receive a free bonus e-book go to www.Iseeyoursoulmate.com/bonus, e-mail her at Sue@Brilliantwork.com, or call 303-939-8574.